DATE DUE			

636.08
WEB

Weber, William J.

Care of uncommon
pets.

716512   01184D

Care of Uncommon Pets

OTHER BOOKS BY WILLIAM J. WEBER

Wild Orphan Babies
Wild Orphan Friends
*Attracting Birds and Other Wildlife
to Your Yard*

CARE OF UNCOMMON PETS

Rabbits, Guinea Pigs, Hamsters,
Mice, Rats, Gerbils, Chickens, Ducks,
Frogs, Toads and Salamanders,
Turtles and Tortoises, Snakes and
Lizards, and Budgerigars

William J. Weber, DVM
photographs by the author

Henry Holt and Company / New York

Published by Henry Holt and Company, Inc.,
521 Fifth Avenue, New York, New York 10175.
Distributed in Canada by Fitzhenry & Whiteside Limited,
195 Allstate Parkway, Markham, Ontario L3R 4T8.

Library of Congress Cataloging in Publication Data
Weber, William J.
Care of uncommon pets.
Includes bibliographies and index.
SUMMARY: Gives information on handling, housing,
feeding, breeding, and diseases.
1. Pets—Juvenile literature. [1. Pets] I. Title.
SF416.2.W43   636.08'87   78-14093

ISBN 0-8050-0294-4 (hardcover)
5 7 9 10 8 6
ISBN 0-8050-0320-7 (paperback)
1 3 5 7 9 10 8 6 4 2

Printed in the United States of America

ISBN 0-8050-0294-4 Hardcover
ISBN 0-8050-0320-7 Paperback

*This book is dedicated to Louise, Jan, Barbara,
Debbie, John, William, and all the past
staff members of the Leesburg Veterinary Hospital.
Thank you all for your support and friendship.*

Contents

Introduction

Certain animals have been excluded from this book on pets. Monkeys are not included for several reasons. While various monkeys are offered in some pet shops, I believe the selling and purchase of these creatures is immoral. Even while many species of monkeys are threatened with extinction, the killing of adult females to capture their nursing babies goes on. It is estimated that for each baby monkey that lives to be a year old, nineteen others have died.

Let's not be a part of this. For if pet stores can't sell them, they won't buy them from the unfeeling dealers who traffic in these helpless babies. There are good public health reasons why monkeys are dangerous as pets, but the horrendous losses in capturing and transporting these creatures is reason enough for me to hope that someday the sales of these primates will be banned.

Exotic cats are not included because they are not pets. They are dangerous animals, capable of inflicting a great deal of damage if they become frightened or angry.

Since keeping insects does not appeal to most people, they also are not included. I would suggest that those who wish to study and keep mantises, spiders, crickets, and butterflies read the section on these creatures in Dr. E. P. Dolensek's book, *A Practical Guide to Impractical Pets* (Viking Press). There is good information on the capturing and care of butterflies and moths in W. J. Holland's *The Moth Book* (Dover Publications).

My son John and I keep bees. These productive insects are of immense interest to us, but they can scarcely be called pets. If bees are of interest to you, a good book that describes the details of their housing and care is *The Art and Adventure of Beekeeping* by Ormand and Harry Aebi (Unity Press).

Wild creatures such as raccoons, foxes, and skunks are also not covered in this book. While raccoons, foxes, and skunks can be purchased at some pet stores, please don't do so. These creatures belong in the wild. They don't make good pets. When they get older, they tend to become cranky and unpredictable. Pet raccoons and skunks have exposed some families to such diseases as rabies and leptospirosis. By your purchase of one of these baby animals, you are contributing to and encouraging the harassment and killing of the adults of these species for the purpose of stealing their babies.

There is another reason to leave these animals be. If they don't work out as pets, you can scarcely return them to the wild. They will have little chance to survive. Zoos and wildlife exhibits won't take them. You are left with the choice of keeping the wild thing constantly caged and isolated or destroying it.

In *Wild Orphan Babies*, I recommend that native wild creatures not be kept as pets. I suggested that we help them when they need help, but that always our ultimate goal be to see them again take their place in the wild community; they have the right to freedom just as we do.

However, I feel there are some exceptions to this rule: A toad, frog, lizard, snake, or turtle can be removed from its native environment and kept as a pet provided you give good quality care, feed it properly, and eventually return it to the wild. These creatures can be returned without any period of adjustment or prolonged procedure for reintroduction. This means their stay with you, whether for a week or several years, will usually not be detrimental to them when they are eventually freed.

Budgies, canaries, mice, rats, hamsters, rabbits, and other small creatures are domesticated. They make wonderful pets if you live in an apartment or other place where space is limited. Just because they are small and inexpensive to purchase does not mean they should not receive knowledgeable care and large quantities of affection.

A third group of creatures such as rabbits, chickens, and ducks not only make intriguing pets, but provide a possible source of food as well. In this book, we shall not be concerned with managing a rabbit herd or a laying flock, but rather with how to care for one, or a few, of these creatures in order to ensure that they are healthy and that you can enjoy them as pets. The fact that you have eggs to share with your family is an incidental benefit.

In keeping any animal as a pet you are agreeing to provide for the well-being of another living individual. It is a responsibility. Care involves not only providing the basic necessities of protection, housing, warmth, health care, and food, but also the giving of personal attention and companionship.

Some of the animals we discuss in this book as pets are also used as research animals. As such, they receive the best in health care, diets established for optimum health and long life, a controlled environment, and housing to answer their specific needs. Yet life in these animal colonies is missing something. Only you can provide the individual attention, gentleness, affection, companionship, and love that are important to the well-being of every individual. An animal kept by itself in captivity needs your companionship. Deprived of relationships with others of its own kind, it looks to you, a human, for company and affection.

While kindness and attention are necessities in care, they do not make up for a lack of basic knowledge in the fundamentals of housing and feeding your pet. It requires some effort on your part to find out about and provide the basic requirements. But this need not be a chore if you truly care about the individual you are acquiring.

Housing should be planned—not just to meet the space requirements as given in a chart or to meet basic sanitary needs—but to prevent boredom and to allow for exercise. Space requirements for cages and housing are minimum requirements. To me there can scarcely be a cage that is too large, but there definitely is a cage that is too small. Most people give the matter little thought. They assume that the cage sold in a pet shop with the creature of their choice is adequate. Frequently this is not true. Good quarters can be provided by the use of common sense and a little effort. If specific information is not available, you may always ask yourself, "If I were a ———, would I like to live in this cage?"

In this book the recommendations on feeding are based on information that has been experimentally obtained and proven through generations of care of the creatures in question. This should not limit your feeding to these specifics. Learn all you can about *your* animal as it exists in the wild and offer appropriate foods based on your reading and your personal experience.

Feeding routines will vary considerably with individual animals. Parakeets should always have food available, while nocturnal rodents, such as rats and mice, are fed once daily in the evening; and snakes may eat only once a week or so.

Always note the amount your pet eats at each feeding. Mammals that go a day or more without eating have a problem. Either they are sick, or the food is spoiled or improper. Creatures that overeat have a problem also. Fat animals are sluggish and more susceptible to disease and other problems. Older animals require less food than active and growing young ones.

Regardless of what animal, bird, or reptile you decide upon, your chance of success in raising it is better if you start with a healthy creature in good condition. Pick an active, alert individual that appears sleek, shiny, and handsome. A strong, solid, unblemished body, bright eyes, and an alert curiosity are also marks of a healthy individual.

I hope your experience with whatever creature you choose is interesting and successful. Should your interest wane, find a new home for your creature or set it free. Do not let it wither and die from neglect.

Remember that the behavior of these creatures is based on their instincts and experiences. When one flees, hides, or bites, it is because that appears to it to be the necessary thing to do to survive. Be patient and calm. You must be willing to understand your creature. As Robert Snedigar points out, "Discipline is necessary—not for the animal, but for the human, thoroughly irrational temper."

1 / Rabbits

A native wild rabbit seldom makes a good pet. Wary and shy, rabbits try to hide and have a strong instinct to flee when alarmed. These basic traits, which protect them so well in their wild environment, are not the traits that make a stable, well-adjusted pet.

A domestic rabbit makes a good pet. Most tame easily. Many can be housebroken, most are docile, and few bite. They are not noisy, although they can make sounds. Older rabbits growl when they do not wish to be bothered, and a panic-stricken rabbit is capable of a loud piercing shriek or scream.

One of the disadvantages of rabbits as pets is that they molt, or lose hair, at certain times of the year. The fall is the usual time for this hair shedding, but some rabbits molt year round. A house rabbit that leaves a trail of hair is seldom appreciated by the one who must clean up after it.

Outdoor rabbits require a hutch for shelter, and all rabbits require some care each day. Since rabbits live for up to fifteen years, they may outlast your interest. Obtaining a rabbit as a pet should not be considered lightly.

Among the twenty-eight different breeds of rabbits, twenty-seven varieties are recognized by the American Rabbit Breeders Association. There are rabbits to suit most individual tastes. There are tiny pygmy rabbits that weigh less than two pounds (.9 kg) and giant breeds that weigh ten times as much. There are black, white, brown, and spotted rabbits with a variety of fur types. Some have soft, long, angoralike coats, but most have shorter ones, with hair about one inch (2.5 cm) long.

Some domestic rabbits look quite similar to wild native cottontails. However, native cottontails are of the genus *Sylvilagus*, while all of the domestic rabbits have the specific name *Oryctolagus cuniculus*. Our domestic rabbits are descendants of the European wild rabbit, which has been raised by man in that part of the world since the 1600s.

Rabbits are classified as lagomorphs, which means "formed like a hare." However, hares, which include jack rabbits, are quite different. Hare babies are born fully furred with their eyes open. Shortly after birth they are able to run and can find food for themselves. Baby rabbits, including the wild cottontail, are born without hair, and their eyes do not open until they are ten days old. They are dependent upon their mother for food and for protection against rain and cold.

A mother rabbit is called a doe, the male is called a buck, and a baby is a bunny. A bunny is usually ready to be weaned and to leave its mother when it is about four weeks old. This is an ideal age for it to become a pet. Bunnies are most attractive at this age, and most easily tamed.

Handling

A bunny just weaned and taken from its mother and littermates is easy to tame. Reach gently into the box or cage and place your hand beside the bunny. Let it smell your hand. Let it get used to your hand's being in the cage or box with it. When the bunny is calm and accepts your hand, gently stroke its side or back. Most rabbits enjoy being petted and soon seem to look forward to it.

Some rabbits enjoy being scratched gently around the base of the ears; others would rather you didn't touch their ears. Although the ears look like excellent handles, under no circumstances are they to be used for carrying a rabbit. It is painful. The rabbit will struggle to escape and will damage the fragile blood vessels in the ears or do even more damage to itself.

Pick your rabbit up by taking hold of a handful of the loose skin over the shoulders. As you begin lifting, using the skin as a handle, slide your other hand under both back feet and support the body weight by allowing the bunny more or less to stand on your hand.

The proper way to lift a bunny.

In this position the rabbit can be carried, lifted into its cage or hutch, or placed on your lap to be petted. When you carry a rabbit, keep the back feet facing away from your body or face. If the rabbit is startled, it may kick with the back feet which have sharp toenails that can scratch.

Under no circumstances should you grasp a rabbit with both hands around its middle and try to lift it. It will always struggle. You will probably be scratched, and as the rabbit thrashes to free itself it may injure its back.

If you have to take your rabbit to a veterinarian for any reason, remember that a rabbit is very uncomfortable on a smooth, slippery surface such as an examination table top. Take an old towel along and place it on the table before you lift your rabbit onto the table. If it still seems nervous, cover its eyes with a portion of the towel. If necessary, gently wrap it in the towel to restrain it.

Careful handling and quiet gentleness will tame most rabbits quickly.

Housing

Even a pet rabbit that you intend to give house privileges to must have a cage or hutch. It should have the security of its own home at night, when you go on vacations, and at other times when it's not convenient for it to be free.

The New Zealand White is probably the most popular rabbit adopted as a pet. As an adult it weighs eight to twelve pounds (4–5 kg). A rabbit this size requires a hutch with a minimum of a square yard (1 square meter) of floor space. A much better size would be a hutch six feet (2 meters) long, two feet (60 cm) wide, and eighteen inches (45 cm) tall.

It need not be elaborate, but certain general basic points must be considered. The hutch can be outside year round. Rabbits tolerate cool temperatures better than hot. Choose a shady spot for sun protection and a spot where some protection from the wind is offered during the winter months. Rabbits do best in a hutch that has a wide mesh bottom. Mesh allows the pelletlike droppings and the urine to fall through and out of the hutch. To make cleaning up the droppings and working in the hutch easier, it should be on legs that raise the cage about twelve to eighteen inches (30–45 cm) above the ground. The raised hutch also offers more protection against foxes and other predators.

Rabbits gnaw, so all major wooden parts of the hutch should be protected with wire. At least two sides should be covered with wire to allow adequate ventilation. The top should be solid and covered with a material that will protect the rabbit from rain and snow.

You can build a hutch. A basic framework is constructed of lumber called 2 × 2s.

The bottom mesh must be sturdy enough to support the weight of your rabbit. You may use galvanized wire—called hardware-cloth—with either a half-inch or five-eighths-inch mesh, or a welded wire with half-inch by inch openings. Either of these materials can be obtained from a hardware or lumber supply store.

The open sides can be made of the same material nailed to the 2 × 2 frame, or a material with larger openings can be used. A welded wire with one-inch by two-inch openings makes excellent sides that are strong enough to resist the teeth of any predator that might try to steal your rabbit.

It is best to make the back side of the hutch of solid boards or plywood. This protects the rabbit from blowing rain and cold winter winds if the hutch is positioned with the solid side facing the prevailing winds.

A door may be built into the front side, or the whole roof can be hinged to the back boards. If the top is hinged, it can be raised to provide access to the entire hutch area for cleaning, feeding, and handling. A prop can be built into the cage to hold the top up.

The hutch should have a wooden shelf in one corner as a resting place for the rabbit. This can be a board six by twelve inches (15 × 30 cm) that rests right on the hardware-cloth bottom. A welded wire rack for feeding hay and grass should be

A piece of wire fence bent into a "V" shape makes a good rabbit hay rack.

Bunny in cage with hardware-cloth sides, sipper-tube waterer, and stainless steel feed dish.

made. It need not be large. Six by twelve inches (15 × 30 cm) will do. Tack it to the back wall where the rabbit can reach it.

A bowl should be placed in the hutch to hold the food. A bowl may also be used for water. These bowls should be heavy with a firm base, so the rabbit does not turn them over, spilling the food and water. I use a sipper-tube water bottle fastened to the side of the cage instead of a water dish.

If you live in a cold climate or have a female you intend to breed, place a nest box in the hutch. A nest box has a solid floor and sides, and a solid removable top. The nest box should be twice as long as the adult rabbit and as wide as the rabbit is long. The sides should be eight inches (20 cm) high. Cut an opening in one side large enough for an entrance. In cold weather a little hay can be provided in the nest box for bedding. At other times of the year, the nest box offers a quiet, cool resting spot.

If you have more than one rabbit, each must have a separate hutch. Males begin fighting soon after weaning. Even a male and a female kept together may fight. Certainly males and females kept together will breed, and while rabbits do not reproduce as rapidly as legend has it, production of baby bunnies can be fast enough to overwhelm a pet owner.

Remember that rabbits are more comfortable at a lower

Rabbit waterer and nest box—large enough for the adult rabbit to turn around in and to stretch out and rest.

temperature than is comfortable for you. They need protection from heat much more than from cold, and shade must be provided. Only in the coldest climate is any extra heat needed if the rabbit has a nest box, and that extra heat would be used in the nest box only if you are expecting baby bunnies.

If you are going to supply heat for the babies, it may be done in several ways. You can replace the flat top of the nest box with an A-frame, or tepee, top. From the peak of such a top, suspend a 40-watt light bulb which does not touch the wood or come in contact with any nest material. A 40-watt bulb suspended twelve inches or so above the nest will supply the needed heat.

Another way to provide heat is to suspend a 150-watt infrared heat lamp from the ceiling of the hutch. The radiant heat falls on the nest box, and as the wood of the sides and top becomes warm, so will the nest inside.

Whenever you supply extra heat, you *must* place a thermometer in the nest box. Do not allow the temperature in the nest box to exceed 60°F (15°C). When the temperature in the nest box is 50° to 60°F (10°–15°C), the nest inside the box will be warmer and the babies will be comfortable. Overheating the babies will not only make them uncomfortable, but can kill them.

If the nest box becomes too warm, use a smaller bulb inside the nest box or move the infrared heat lamp farther from the nest box. *Be safe*; monitor the temperature carefully until you know it is stable with the heat source you are using.

The droppings that pass through the hutch bottom accumulate and can attract flies. They should be cleaned up weekly and spread around the shrubbery and flowers where they help these plants by acting as fertilizer. Scattering the droppings eliminates the attraction for flies.

Rabbits normally use one particular spot in the hutch to urinate and defecate. This fact is what makes it possible to housebreak most rabbits. If you allow your pet rabbit the limited freedom of a porch or a single room, it will pick one spot where it will eliminate. Place several thicknesses of newspaper at this spot and liberally cover the papers with sand, dirt, or kitty litter. Clean up the litter and soiled papers as needed and replace with fresh material.

As the rabbit becomes accustomed to using this specific spot, you can substitute an aluminum tray or plastic dishpan with sand or litter in it. Cut one of the sides down to provide an easy entrance. As your pet becomes more dependable about using its pan, you can allow it into other rooms in the house.

While rabbits are fastidious in their habits and do pick one spot to eliminate, a few just never seem to acquire this habit. If you have one of the careless types, I know of no way to train it to be neat. It should be an outside pet, not a house bunny.

Feeding

Rabbits are *herbivorous*. They will eat most types of greens, grains, hay, and vegetables. They can be fed table scraps and vegetable trimmings. There are complete diets available as a pelleted food. These rabbit pellets can be obtained at most pet stores and all feed stores.

Our pet rabbits have been maintained on a combination of rabbit pellets and table scraps. We feed all the good vegetable trimmings, bread crusts, and other items relished by a rabbit. We offer the rabbit pellets, too. We also feed grass trimmings, hay when we have it, and even weeds pulled from the shrubbery and the garden.

If you are going to follow this way of feeding, there are several things to keep in mind. Feed each variety of food consistently, not just once in a while. A rabbit will overeat on fresh greens if it has not been receiving them regularly. This frequently causes diarrhea.

Rabbit pellets have all the essential food elements, so no supplementary foods are required. However, if you feed mostly table foods, you must supplement the diet with salt. Salt blocks and spools are available. Blocks are placed in the rabbit cage on the floor, and a salt spool can be wired to the side of the cage. The rabbit will lick either one to obtain the salt it needs.

Because a rabbit's teeth grow continuously, it must chew to

keep them worn down. It is a good idea to place a hardwood block four by four by ten inches (10 × 10 × 25 cm) or several hardwood limbs in the hutch to provide chewing exercise. Dry hay and grass provide a nutritional tooth-wearing food.

An adult rabbit will usually eat a half to one ounce (14–28 grams) of food per pound (.45 kg) of body weight each day. An adult New Zealand White would eat about one quarter to one half pound (10–25 grams) daily. Some adult rabbits, if fed all they want, may become too fat.

Weigh your rabbit regularly. Weigh yourself on the scale, then weigh yourself while holding your rabbit. Write the difference in the two weights on your calendar or in some other handy log. By comparing these weights, you can be sure your young rabbit is gaining weight and your adult pet is maintaining a consistent weight. A sudden loss of weight in an adult is cause for alarm, and your pet should be examined by a veterinarian. A steady increase in weight in an adult means you must cut down on the amount you are feeding until a steady weight is maintained.

Feeding utensils and dishes should be kept clean. They should be washed as needed. Even if they look clean, they should be thoroughly washed weekly. Clean the area under the cage weekly, too.

Fresh clean water must be available at all times. A rabbit will normally drink one to two ounces (30–60 ml) per pound (.45 kg) of body weight per day. A mature New Zealand White would drink up to a pint (half a liter) a day. But in hot weather it may drink three times that much. Not having adequate water available in hot weather condemns your rabbit to a tragic death.

Rabbits are most active at night. While they can be fed at any time, it is probably best to feed them late in the afternoon. Then food is available during their most active time. Also the succulent foods will not spoil as readily in the cool of the day.

All rabbits eat some of their droppings. This is called *coprophagy*. The wire floors of the hutch do not eliminate or cut down on this instinctive habit.

In the early morning the rabbits produce a softer pellet

covered with mucus, which they swallow as it is passed from the anus. This is a form of recycling. The rabbit obtains vitamins produced by intestinal bacteria and additional protein broken down by these bacteria. While not pleasant by our standards, this coprophagy serves an important function in rabbit nutrition.

Breeding

When you acquire your rabbit it is possible to determine what sex it is. If you obtain your rabbit from a commercial breeder, he will show you how to tell the difference. If your rabbit comes from a pet shop or you are selecting one from a friend's litter, you may be on your own in determining its sex. To do so, pick it up by the skin over the shoulders and support the feet as usual. Then place the back of the rabbit against your stomach. Gradually remove the hand that supports the feet until the rabbit is hanging from your hand next to your body. With your free hand, gently stroke the rabbit's chest and stomach. It will relax completely. This is a form of vertical hypnosis, and will allow the underside of the rabbit to be examined thoroughly while it stays still and quiet. The genital opening will be just below the rectum or anus on the lower abdomen. If you place your thumb on one side of the opening and a finger on the other, you can gently press and spread this slitlike opening. In a buck the opening is round and a tiny penis protrudes as you gently press the area around the opening. In the doe, or female, the opening is a longer slit and there is no penis.

Choose a female for a pet, since bucks tend to get cantankerous as they get older. The female is a potential breeder if you decide you wish a litter of bunnies. Most females will be mature enough to breed when they are six to nine months of age. The smaller breeds mature earlier than the larger breeds.

Customarily the female is placed in the male's cage when she is to be bred. Most rabbits will breed anytime of the year, and *ovulation* is triggered by the act of breeding.

If you obtained your pet from a rabbit breeder, contact him if you decide to breed your doe. He has bucks available and can select a suitable mate for your rabbit. Most bucks will mate with the female within a minute or two after she is placed in the cage. After mating, remove the doe from the buck's cage. Rebreeding, a practice of some breeders, is not necessary.

If the female refuses to accept the buck, she can be removed and brought back to try again a couple of days later. If she will not accept the male or allow him to breed, she may be held or restrained until he can do so.

After breeding the female is returned to her hutch. She should have a nest box. Give her some clean hay, straw, or well-dried grass clippings to use for nest material. Her abdomen will get noticeably larger in two weeks. Baby bunnies can be expected in thirty to thirty-two days. This is the *gestation period* for the domestic rabbit. At about the twenty-eighth day of gestation, she will begin to pull hair from her lower abdomen and chest to line her nest. When she does this you will know that it is almost time for the new bunnies.

The act of giving birth is called "kindling" in rabbits. The doe should not be disturbed at kindling, for a nervous doe may trample and kill the tiny newborn bunnies. Since new mothers lack experience, any bunnies born outside the nest box must be retrieved and placed in the nest box by you.

The next day, when the doe is not in the nest box, you can remove the lid of the nest box and gently open the soft furry nest to check the baby bunnies. The usual litter is about eight. If the babies are all right they should be left alone until the next day. Check the nest box daily. Any dead bunnies should be removed from the nest.

A newborn New Zealand bunny weighs about three and a half ounces (100 grams), is pink, hairless, and its eyes are sealed closed. At three weeks of age the babies will begin to venture out of the nest box and will nibble on food placed in the hutch for the mother. At one month they will be eating well. Bunnies should be weaned at six to eight weeks of age. Weaning is less difficult for the bunnies if they are allowed to stay in their familiar hutch, and the mother rabbit is moved to a new home.

If you have decided to breed rabbits, the female should be

rebred when she is removed to her new hutch. This is an important decision and should not be made unless you have a market for your rabbits. A female is capable of producing six litters of nine or ten bunnies each in a year's time. As you can see, a number of hutches will be required in a short time.

A group of producing rabbits is called a herd. Herd size refers to the number of mature breeding does, not bunnies or bucks. Most breeders keep only one buck for each ten or fifteen does. The surplus bucks must be sold. Bucks must be kept in separate hutches, for they frequently begin fighting before they are even weaned.

In breeding rabbits there are a few difficulties to be aware of. False pregnancy is a problem in some does. If your doe begins pulling hair and making a nest at three weeks after breeding instead of four weeks, she probably is not bred but is going through a false pregnancy. She should be returned to the buck and be rebred at once.

Rabbits will breed year round, but bucks are reluctant to breed in hot weather. Conception is lowest in fall and winter and highest in spring and early summer.

If your litter has twelve or more bunnies, it is too large. Some baby bunnies in a litter of this size usually die. If you have another doe with a smaller litter, you can give her some of the bunnies from the larger litter, for does will accept foster babies. You can take several of the babies from a large litter and hand raise them. This requires a lot of time and work, even though the bunnies are fed only twice daily.

Take one large egg yolk and enough homogenized milk to make two-thirds of a cupful and mix it well. This formula will provide an adequate diet. Newborn babies will take about one teaspoon (5 ml) of formula the first day. This increases until they take up to two to three tablespoons (20–45 ml) a day by weaning age. This formula may be fed with a medicine dropper or a pet nurser bottle. As with human infants, all utensils must be kept scrupulously clean. The formula must be kept refrigerated, and only the amount to be used at a single feeding should be poured from refrigerated supply and warmed.

A program of breeding rabbits doesn't just happen. You must be an observant student of rabbit behavior, and you must read to learn about a rabbit's needs and requirements. A successful herd demonstrates that you care about your charges.

Diseases

Most disease problems in rabbits are problems common to a herd. Single pet rabbits have few disease problems. Most rabbits are healthy and are easily cared for. The problems mentioned here 'are those that veterinarians see in pet rabbits.

Ear Mites: These are small insects similar to tiny spiders that live and reproduce in the ear canal. An infested ear may contain hundreds of these mites. They irritate the lining of the ear canal. Tissue fluids combined with normal ear secretions, and the debris of the mite infection produces a smelly, dark-colored discharge that fills the entire ear. The ear droops. The rabbit scratches at the ear and shakes its head.

Apply a liberal amount of mineral oil or olive oil to both ear canals at least twice weekly. Gently massage the ear to help the oil penetrate into the debris. The oil smothers the mites. It also softens the waxy discharge, cleans the ear, and protects the lining of the ear canal.

It is not necessary to pick the material out of the ear. It is necessary to treat the ears twice a week for one month. Treatment should be done out of doors, for the rabbit will shake both oil and debris out of the ears as soon as you turn it loose.

Diarrhea: Normally a rabbit eliminates well-formed pellets of bowel material. Soft, runny bowel material is diarrhea. There are many causes of diarrhea in young rabbits. If a virulent infection is involved, young rabbits die before any treatment can be started. Overeating on green foods the rabbit isn't used to can cause diarrhea. Cutting back on the amount of greens offered each day may be all that is needed to correct the condition.

If the diarrhea persists for more than a day, have a veterinarian check your pet. Diarrhea caused by bacterial infection is usually treated with antibiotics, which he will prescribe.

Paralysis of Rear Legs: In this condition the rabbit is not able to use its rear legs. It can pull itself along the floor but is not able to stand or walk. Frequently this is the sequel to improper handling. In the rabbit's struggle to free itself, muscles of the back are torn in mild cases, or the back may be fractured in severe cases. The back can be X-rayed to determine the extent of the injury.

Where X-ray is not available, keep the rabbit as still as possible for the next three weeks. Place food and water where it can reach them. If the rabbit is not able to use the legs at the end of the three weeks, the injury is usually permanent. *Euthanasia* is the humane course to follow.

Heatstroke: Rabbits must be kept cool. During hot weather, particularly when the humidity is high, your rabbit may begin panting. Cool it down right away. Set up a hose so a fine mist is sprayed on the rabbit and the hutch. Place a milk carton of ice or a cloth bag of ice cubes in the hutch on warm days.

If the rabbit isn't cooled down, it may continue panting and drooling until it becomes exhausted. It is unable to walk and soon passes into a coma. Treatment started at this stage is usually too late.

Buck Teeth or Malocclusion: A rabbit's incisor teeth grow continuously. It must have hay, wood, or other material to chew on in order to keep the teeth worn down. If it doesn't, the teeth become long, twisted, and grow past each other, and the rabbit is unable to eat.

There is an inherited condition in rabbits in which the lower incisors grow out in front of the uppers. Since there is no wear, the teeth soon grow overly long.

The treatment for both of these conditions is to cut off the extra length of the incisors. A cutting pliers may be used. No anesthetic is necessary, for the teeth contain no nerves. Your veterinarian can show you how to cut off the teeth properly.

Providing chewing materials will prevent the teeth from overgrowing again in most cases. In the others, repeated trimming is necessary to control the growth of the teeth.

Pregnancy Toxemia: This condition sometimes appears in fat does at the time of kindling or shortly afterward. It is a serious condition, and even with veterinary treatment some does die.

The doe is found lying comatose (stiff and lifeless) in the hutch. Veterinarians treat this condition by injecting 10 ml of a 50 percent glucose solution intravenously.

If no veterinarian is available, you can try to treat your rabbit. Since you cannot give the intravenous medication, you can try to give a sugar solution orally. This sugar solution must be one that can be absorbed from the doe's intestinal tract without having to be digested. Therefore, you must use what is called a simple sugar, such as glucose. Honey contains a simple sugar. If glucose is not available, you may make the proper solution by adding one teaspoon (5 cc) of honey to two tablespoons (30 ml) of water.

Since the doe is comatose, it cannot swallow. The prepared solution must be given with a stomach tube. A veterinarian could provide a tube and show you how to do it easily, but since this is an emergency treatment when no veterinarian is available, you will have to improvise.

A plastic eighth- or quarter-inch (3–6 mm) tube about twelve inches (30 cm) long may be used as the stomach tube. You will also need a syringe—a plastic food dispenser (such as a mustard or ketchup dispenser) or a bulb syringe (such as a turkey or meat baster)—to hold the medication and force it through the tubing into the rabbit's stomach. The dispenser must fit on, or into, the end of the stomach tube.

Put the medication into the dispenser and place it close at hand. Lay the doe on a table on her left side with her head pointed to your right. Measure from the rabbit's last rib to its nose and mark this distance on your tube. This is the distance the tube will be inserted.

Lubricate the outside of the stomach tube with a little margarine or butter, so it will pass more easily. Placing the thumb and first finger of one hand on each side of the mouth, gently force the rabbit's mouth slightly open. Gently push the tube into the back part of the mouth. If it hits an obstruction and doesn't go down, withdraw it a little way and start down again. In a few tries the tube will enter the throat. When your mark on the tube reaches the rabbit's nose, you know the end is in the stomach.

Attach your dispenser to the tube and gently and slowly expel the medication through the tube into the rabbit's stomach. Slowly remove the tube.

Keep the rabbit warm and quiet. If it is still alive, but not up and about, repeat this procedure again in one hour.

If the doe recovers, it should receive a teaspoonful of sugar in each pint of water you place in its waterer for the next five or six days.

Upper Respiratory Infection: The usual signs of upper respiratory infection are sneezing, coughing, and a mucous discharge from eyes and nose. This is usually a bacterial infection. In a herd, it is most frequently caused by a Pasteurella organism and is called snuffles. Untreated, this condition can extend to a middle ear infection, pneumonia, and death.

Rabbits usually accept medication from a medicine dropper. A rabbit should receive 80 mg of an antibiotic per kilogram of body weight each day. This is divided into several doses. Panmycin (Upjohn Co.) contains 100 mgs of tetracycline in each ml. This product has a measuring dropper to give the proper dosage and is available from your veterinarian. If your pet is too sick, he may suggest treating the infection by an injection of antibiotic.

Rabbit Fever-Tularemia: Many people have heard of this disease in wild rabbits. It does not occur in domestic rabbits and is no problem to your pet.

Cuterebra Warbles: This disease is not common in most pet rabbits. It is caused by a fly larva that burrows into the skin. It is noticed as a swelling in the skin with a hole in the center. The end of the larval worm can be seen in the hole. The hole must be enlarged with a sharp blade or scissors. The larva can then be removed with a forceps. The hole heals quickly.

Internal Parasites: Rabbits can get internal parasites such as roundworms, tapeworms, and coccidia. If you see what you believe are worms being passed by your pet, collect several specimens in a plastic vial and let your veterinarian examine them. It is a good idea to take eight or ten bowel pellets in another vial for microscopic examination at the same time. Your veterinarian will identify the parasites and prescribe the specific medication needed.

Because rabbits are large, they require a larger cage and larger facilities than some other pets. They are totally dependent upon you for their well being and care, and you must realize that you accept this responsibility when you accept a rabbit as a pet.

References and Suggested Reading

Dolensek, Emil P., and Barbara Burn. *A Practical Guide to Impractical Pets.* New York: Viking Press, 1976.

Domestic Rabbits: Diseases and Parasites. Agricultural Handbook No. 490, U.S.D.A., 1976.

Nutrient Requirements of Rabbits. Publication 1194, National Academy of Science, Washington, D.C., 1966.

Weber, William J. *Wild Orphan Babies.* New York: Holt, Rinehart & Winston, 1975.

Williams, Christine. *Practical Guide to Laboratory Animals.* St. Louis: C. V. Mosby Co., 1976.

2 / Guinea Pigs

Guinea pigs can make ideal pets. They are quite small, rarely bite or scratch, and require minimum care and housing. They are relatively quiet and enjoy being handled and petted.

The popular name for this creature is cavy. Its scientific name is *Cavia porcellus*. But most of us know this little, tailless creature simply as the guinea pig. They were originally called pigs because of the soft grunts, squeals, and whistling sounds they make. But while they do learn to chirp for attention and at feeding time frequently whistle, they are quiet most of the time. The "guinea" part of their name comes from the fact that in England, when they were first brought to that country from Peru, they were sold for an English coin called a guinea.

The guinea pig has been used in nutritional and disease research for over one hundred years, and has been appreciated as a pet for as long. There are three recognized breeds: American cavy, Abyssinian cavy, and Peruvian cavy. Of the three, the

American cavy is best known. While it comes in a variety of colors, it is usually white and has a short smooth-hair coat. The Abyssinian cavy is similar in size and color, but it has a harsh, wiry short-hair coat. Growth patterns of hair appear as rosettes over the body and neck. The Peruvian cavy is about the same size as the others, but looks larger, for it has a long, silky-hair coat up to six inches (15 cm) in length.

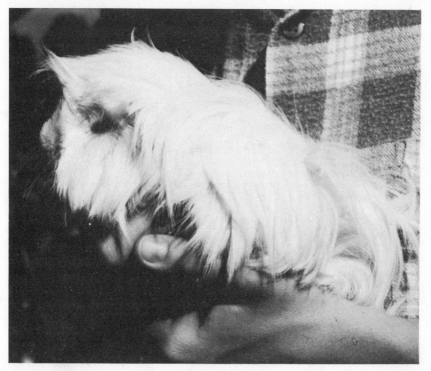

Peruvian cavy.

Mature guinea pigs seldom weigh more than two pounds (.9 kg). Babies weigh only two to three ounces (60–90 grams) when born. They grow rapidly. By four or five weeks of age they weigh half a pound (240 grams), and they are mature enough to breed at three to four months of age. When healthy, they live to be eight or nine years old.

Guinea pigs are odorless, gentle, easy to tame and handle, and they seem to appreciate attention.

Handling

Guinea pigs tame easily. The only requirement for taming is that you spend time with them. They look forward to the attention and chirp happily when you appear, if you have been kind and gentle to them.

To pick up a small young guinea pig, cup both your hands around it and slide them under it. The guinea pig can stand in the saucerlike depression of your hands. It won't bite or scratch, so there is no danger to you. But be sure it doesn't jump or fall from your hands, for a fall certainly would hurt it.

An older, larger guinea pig can be picked up by circling its chest with the fingers of one hand while you support the back part by sliding the other hand under its bottom. Older animals that haven't been handled much will wiggle and squirm. Hold them just firmly enough so that they don't escape, but be sure not to squeeze them.

The proper way to pick up an older, larger guinea pig.

If the guinea pig is in a cage and has not been handled, it will run away from you. As you try to grasp it, it will frequently squeak and squeal, because it is frightened. Be gentle. Since this timid creature doesn't jump or climb, it is easy to use your hands to herd it into a corner, then to catch it. And since it doesn't usually bite or scratch, handle it in a fashion that is comfortable and reassuring to this shy little animal.

While it doesn't take long to tame a guinea pig, it will not stay tame unless you spend some time with it each day.

Housing

Housing for guinea pigs need not be elaborate, since they won't climb and can't jump higher than an inch or so. However, they must be protected from extreme heat and cold. They do best at 65° to 75°F (18°–24°C), the temperatures most comfortable to us.

A guinea pig does not require a large cage. A cage bottom ten by twenty inches (25 × 50 cm) with screened sides ten inches (25 cm) high is adequate. A cage twice as large would make the guinea pig more content by allowing it more room for exercise.

The bottom of the cage should be solid and constructed of boards or plywood suitable for exterior use. If guinea pigs are kept in wire-floored cages, leg injuries can occur. The sides of the cage can be made of small wire mesh or hardware-cloth. This heavy, screenlike material allows air to circulate in the cage and also holds in the bedding material.

Guinea pigs like lots of bedding. The bedding may be any absorbent material. Wood chips, hay, dried grass clippings, even shredded newspaper can be used. Add at least one inch of this material each time you give the cage its weekly cleaning. The top of the cage may be made of boards and hinged to the back side, or it can be of hardware-cloth in a wood frame fastened the same way.

If the cage is kept indoors, where your guinea pig is protected from dog and cat predators, it need not have a top. If you wish to allow your pet to graze on the lawn on the warmer

Guinea pig in wire cage with large mesh on bottom, so it can graze while protected from dogs and cats.

Guinea pig in roomy cage with hay, food, and sipper-tube waterer.

days, you can use the same cage by turning it upside down on the grass. This provides security, confinement, and shade while giving your friend a change in diet and atmosphere.

If you don't wish to lose the bedding each time you offer your guinea pig grazing privileges, make a separate portable outdoor cage. Be sure the cage is light enough to be easily moved, secure enough to protect your friend from wandering dogs and cats, and that part of the top is solid so as to provide shade protection from the hot sun, unless you keep it in the shade.

The permanent cage must have a water bottle to provide clean water at all times and a feeding dish that cannot be tipped over easily.

Other "luxury" items can be added to make your pet happier. A wooden shelf four by eight inches (10×20 cm) in one corner of the cage fastened securely about three inches (8 cm) from the floor will make a perch it can climb upon to nap and rest. A covered sleeping or nest box slightly larger than the shelf can be placed in another corner. Guinea pigs need a place to hide if frightened, and enjoy having a quiet, dark spot for naps during the day.

Like other rodents, they enjoy and need to chew to keep their teeth properly worn down. Put several hardwood branches up to two or three inches (6–8 cm) in diameter on the floor of the cage. The branches will tend to hold the bedding in place and provide excellent chewing sticks. They can also be used as scratching posts to keep the toenails from getting too long.

Feeding

Guinea pigs are vegetarians. They will eat almost all green, leafy vegetables, carrots and corn, fruits such as apples, peaches, grapes, and tomatoes, grains, and whole wheat bread. They will also eat lawn clippings, dandelions, and other weeds removed from your garden or shrubbery.

Guinea pigs can be fed rabbit pellets. These are small compressed pellets of hay mixed with other foods to make a balanced and complete diet for a rabbit. They can be obtained from any feed store or pet shop and can be on the basis of a guinea pig diet. However—and this is important—guinea pigs must have additional vitamin C daily. Most animals can make vitamin C in their own bodies. Guinea pigs cannot, so you must provide this vitamin in their food. When rabbit pellets are your basic diet, give a green, leafy vegetable and a little fruit along with the pellets each day, since vitamin C is found in these foods.

A guinea pig can get along very well on the foods that are left over from your table. All that is required is that you provide a variety of foods of the type mentioned along with a couple of supplements. If the diet is going to be whole wheat bread with vegetable and fruit trimmings, provide extra salt as the first supplement. Salt is available in small blocks or spools from feed and pet shops. As the second supplement, provide fatty acids not found in most vegetable foods by giving your pet one teaspoonful (5 cc) of corn oil on part of the food offered.

Hay is nutritionally not necessary, but should be given if possible. It provides chewing exercise and gives the guinea pig an activity that keeps it busy and content. The hay also provides additional bedding and something to crawl under when there is a wish to hide.

Baby guinea pigs can eat solid foods from the day they are born. Orphaned baby guinea pigs can usually survive even with no milk or formula, but providing it makes raising orphans easier. The formula of one-half cup of homogenized milk with one egg yolk mixed in it works well. Baby guinea pigs and very young animals receive the same diets that adults receive.

Guinea pigs will usually eat one and one-half ounces of food for each pound that they weigh. If your pet quickly cleans up all the food you give, you are probably not feeding it enough. If quite a bit of food is left when you feed the next day, or your guinea pig is beginning to take the shape of a soft ball, you should cut down on the amount you are feeding.

Many guinea pigs have a bad habit of eliminating in their food and water dishes. For this reason both dishes must be changed or washed regularly each day.

Using a water bottle instead of a dish helps avoid part of this problem, but can lead to another. As they play, some guinea pigs chew the sipper tube and blow air mixed with saliva back into the bottle. The water quickly becomes cloudy, bad smelling, and contains floating bits of food and hay. Obviously, such a water bottle must be changed frequently.

Guinea pigs will drink two to three ounces (60–90 ml) of water daily. They will drink three or four times this much if they are not receiving green vegetables—which also supply liquid—regularly.

Breeding

Although guinea pigs are mature enough to breed when they are three to five months old, they should not be bred until they are at least five months of age. A female who is to be bred, should be bred at this age.

In young female guinea pigs, called sows, the bones of the pelvis have not united completely at the area called the symphysis. This allows the pelvic bones to spread during the birth process, giving more room for the passage of babies.

If a female guinea pig is not bred until it is seven or eight months or a year old, the pelvic opening has usually become inflexible. This means the babies cannot pass through the pelvis no matter how hard the female strains, and no babies are born. Unless a *Cesarean section* is performed by your veterinarian, which is expensive, death is certain in these older sows with a first litter.

If the sow has been bred regularly, the birth process keeps the pelvis from uniting solidly by periodically stretching the tissues of the area. For these reasons, it you decide to breed your pet, do it while she is young but old enough to be mature. Males can be bred at any age after they are mature.

A sow can have as many as four or five litters a year. However, once she has not been bred or had babies for six months or a year, do not breed her again.

To be bred, a female is usually placed in the pen with the male. She is receptive to breeding every sixteen to nineteen days. If you have both the male and the female, you may just leave them together until you see them breeding and then place the female back in her cage; or you can leave the male with the female throughout the pregnancy period. Male guinea pigs, called boars, don't harm the babies and are accepted by the sows.

Ovulation occurs at the time of breeding and in sixty-three to seventy days you can expect babies. Some females become so large during the last weeks of their pregnancy that they can't stand or walk. Don't handle them at this time. Place their food and water where they can reach it. Clean up wet and dirty bedding from around them as needed.

The babies are born fully haired and with their eyes open. There may be from one to six in the litter, but most often there are three or four. Don't handle the babies the first day or disturb the mother too much, for a panicky, stampeding mother can trample and kill the newborn.

However, if you intend to breed her again the time to do it is now: the same day that her babies are born. She can be placed in the male's pen for a short period. If the male has been left with her during the pregnancy period, they will breed soon after the babies are born.

The baby guinea pigs nurse from the mother and begin eating food on their own almost at once. They can be weaned by the time they are three or four weeks of age, for they are eating well by this time.

At weaning time the babies can be examined to determine if they are males or females. Hold the baby gently around the chest with one hand and allow it to hang vertically from your hand, so that you can see and inspect its underside. Look closely at the genital area. The animals with Y-shaped folds are females. The males have a short straight slit in this area. You can verify that they are males by feeling the abdomen just forward of the slit with the tip of one finger. In the males, the penis will feel like a small matchstick under the skin.

Diseases

Vitamin C Deficiency: Guinea pigs who are not receiving adequate vitamin C look terrible. Their fur coat is rough, matted, and sticks out every which way. They can't walk well, because the joints in their legs are swollen and painful. Tiny hemorrhages appear under the skin and membranes of the mouth. They frequently have diarrhea and will die unless the diet is corrected.

In critical cases a veterinarian will give the deficient animal 50 mg of vitamin C daily. But, most often, correcting the diet to provide fresh fruits and vegetables is all that is needed.

Dry Scaly Skin and Loss of Hair: This can be due to a deficiency of fatty acids or specific amino acids or to a fungus infection.

Your guinea pig should be given a teaspoonful (5 cc) of corn oil daily in its food. In addition, provide additional foods to allow for more variety in the diet.

If the skin has not dramatically improved in thirty days, have your guinea pig checked by a veterinarian for dermatomycosis (fungus infection). Several tests can be performed, and if fungus is diagnosed, it is usually treated by giving 10 mg of gruseofulvin per pound (22 mg per kg) of body weight daily in the food for a month.

Hair Loss with Healthy Normal Skin: Patches on the rear quarters where the hair appears to be clipped short are the result of "self-barbering" by the guinea pig. Usually this is due to boredom. Provide hay for chewing and large sticks for gnawing, and the hair will grow back.

Loss of hair on the sides and back that makes the hair coat look very thin occurs frequently in pregnant guinea pigs. This does not usually occur if the female has hay available. In any event, the hair will grow back after the babies are born.

Lice or Fleas: This is not a common problem, but if you see pale yellow bugs or tiny brown fleas on your pet, dust it with any flea powder that states on the label that it is safe for cats. Repeat this treatment once a week for three weeks.

Bite Wounds: Male guinea pigs will fight, especially if they are in a cage with females. Wounds in the skin should be treated by applying an antiseptic or antibiotic ointment. The males must be placed in separate cages.

Pregnancy Toxemia: This condition occurs most frequently in fat pregnant females, particularly in the first or second pregnancy. It occurs during the last part of the pregnancy period. The female becomes listless, doesn't eat, becomes unconscious, and will die in less than twenty-four hours. She may be found dead before you are even aware that she was sick.

If toxemia is detected in time, your veterinarian may be able to save the animal by giving a glucose solution intravenously. If no veterinarian is available, prepare a solution of one tea-spoon (5 cc) of honey in two tablespoons (30 ml) of water. This solution can be given orally with a medicine dropper. Give just one drop at a time every two to three minutes as long as you can get her to swallow.

Intestinal Parasites (Worms): This is seldom a problem. If you think your guinea pig has worms because of loose droppings or diarrhea or because you actually see wormlike organisms, take a teaspoonful of fresh droppings and place them in a plastic vial or baggie. Get it to your veterinarian for microscopic examina-tion. Tell him what you saw, or what your pet is doing, that makes you think it has worms.

If internal parasites are diagnosed, he will prescribe a specific medicine for that particular parasite.

Bacterial Pneumonia: The guinea pig will be listless, will eat poorly, and frequently will have a mucous or pus-like discharge from the nose and eyes. The mucous discharge causes the eye-lids to stick together and there will be some sneezing.

Pneumonia is treated with antibiotics, but the choice of the antibiotic is critical. An injection of penicillin, for example, will kill 80 percent of all guinea pigs in three to eight days. Penicillin kills normal beneficial bacteria in the intestinal tract and allows others to grow in their place. This is called a gram-negative bacterial enterotoxemia.

Most veterinarians prefer chloramphenicol. A 250 mg capsule is added to one pint (half a liter) of water. Sweeten the water with a teaspoonful (5 cc) of sugar. This mixture is given as the only water supply in the sipper bottle for the next five days. To get the proper dosage, a one pound (450 gram) guinea pig must be drinking two to three ounces (60–90 ml) of water daily. The mixture may be made more concentrated or more diluted as needed to provide the proper dosage of 45 mg of the drug per pound (100 mg per kg) of guinea pig weight per day.

Lymphadenitis: Commonly called lumps, this disease causes a swelling under the chin along the neck. It is caused by a streptococcal organism and is treated with the antibiotic chloramphenicol in exactly the same way as bacterial pneumonia.

References and Suggested Reading

Clifford, D. R. "What the Practicing Veterinarian Should Know About Guinea Pigs," *VM/SAC*, June 1973, pp. 678–85.

Dolensek, Emil P., and Barbara Burn. *A Practical Guide to Impractical Pets.* New York: Viking Press, 1976.

Nutrient Requirements of Laboratory Animals. National Academy of Sciences. Washington, D.C., 1972.

Williams, Christine. *Practical Guide to Laboratory Animals.* St. Louis: C. V. Mosby Co., 1976.

3 / Hamsters

An adult hamster looks like a miniature teddy bear. It has a plump body, a tiny tail, short stocky legs, small dark ears, and soft reddish-brown fur. The fur on its underside is lighter in color. The hamster is not a large rodent, for it is less than six inches (15 cm) long and weighs from three to six ounces (90–180 grams).

The hamster is one of the few mammals that has cheek pouches. When it has eaten all it can hold, it fills its cheek pouches with remaining food, which it carries to its storehouse. In fact, the name hamster comes from the German word *hamstern,* which means "to hoard." The hamster's scientific name is *Mesocricetus auratus*—"golden rodent."

Hamsters were unknown until 1930, when a Palestinian zoologist found a mother hamster and twelve babies in a burrow under the ground in Syria. All the tame hamsters in the world are descendants of those few individuals found by Professor Aharoni.

The first hamsters came to the United States in 1938. These hardy and prolific creatures, which quickly became popular as laboratory research animals and as pets, have a life span of up to four years.

Handling

Hamsters are not difficult to tame. Ones that haven't been handled can be ferocious until they get to know you and realize that you are a friend. To reach in casually and grasp a hamster that doesn't know you is almost to guarantee a sharp painful bite.

If you must handle an excitable or frightened hamster, wear heavy leather gloves. Cup both gloved hands around the hamster, making a cage of your two hands. The hamster can then be picked up and placed in its cage.

Laboratory personnel often handle strange hamsters and are accustomed to them. They prefer not to wear gloves. Their way of picking up a hamster is to grasp the loose skin at the shoulder firmly between their fingers and carry the hamster by the scruff of the neck. The hamster doesn't like that and will frequently nip if it gets a chance.

The best way for you to handle your new pet hamster is with a clean tin can. Use a number two can that vegetables come in. Remove one end with a can opener and wash the can thoroughly. Place the can on its side in the cage or box. Most hamsters will go in the can at once, for they are curious creatures. Place your hand over the end to keep the hamster in the can. That will allow you to lift or move the hamster easily.

That is your first step in taming your pet. To capture it in a can. Then talk to it softly all the time you are with it, so it will get to know your voice. Sit down on the floor beside the cage and then let the hamster walk out of the can and onto the hand that was blocking the entrance. Let the hamster walk about on both of your hands. It will explore your hands and arms and become acquainted with you. If it gets too active, or it looks as if it might jump or escape, place it back in its cage.

Three or four taming sessions each day will soon make your hamster into a gentle pet. After that, you can discard the can and pick up your friend with your bare hands.

To do so, gently grasp it around its middle with one hand or slide your cupped hands under it. You will soon find which it prefers, for if it is dissatisfied, it will wiggle and struggle to get free.

Your hamster will soon look forward to your company and will allow you to handle it anytime and carry it anywhere. But there are still several points to remember.

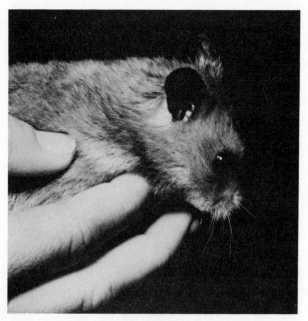

A hamster is content to sit in your hand.

If your hamster is sleeping, be sure you talk to it and wake it up before you grasp it, for a hamster awakened suddenly will almost always bite defensively. It will bite before it recognizes you. So wake it up first. Then when you are sure that it has recognized you, pick it up.

Remember also, the hamster is *your* friend. If a stranger reaches into the cage to pick it up, the hamster may bite. If you wish to have someone handle or pet your hamster, you pick it up and place it in the cupped hands of that person. Your hamster will take a few moments walking about, sniffing, and becoming acquainted with the new person. Then it will usually allow itself to be handled and petted.

Loud noises or sudden movements may startle a hamster. If it is being held, it may become frightened and can bite trying to escape. Anticipate this situation, and don't allow boisterous children to handle your pet or to tease it.

Frequent gentle handling will keep your curious hamster a tractable and enjoyable pet.

Housing

Hamsters are small and do not require large cages. However, they do enjoy chewing and unless the cage is sturdy and well made, they will chew a hole and escape.

The cage should have a solid bottom rather than one of screen or mesh. The minimum cage size for a single hamster would be twelve by sixteen inches (30 × 40 cm), with twelve-inch (30-cm) sides. But a floor area twice that size would be better, for it would give more room for exercise and normal hamster activities. The hamster uses one spot in the cage for storing food, another area for eating, another for sleeping, and another for elimination.

At least two of the sides should be of screen or mesh to allow a good exchange of fresh air. Hardware-cloth is excellent, providing you choose a mesh size small enough to keep the absorbent bedding confined to the inside of the cage. Hardware-cloth sides are firm enough to stand by themselves when fastened to the cage bottom, or they can be tacked to a wooden framework for more rigidity. If a wooden framework is used, the hardware-cloth should be on the inside to prevent the frame from being chewed. See Chapter 13 for cage construction details.

This hardware-cloth cage is large enough for a single hamster, but a solid bottom on the cage would be better.

The top may be of hardware-cloth also, or a wooden top may be hinged to the framework. Regardless of how you make your cage, be sure the top fits well.

The entire floor area should be covered with at least one inch of absorbent material. Sawdust, wood chips, shredded newspapers, dried grass, or hay can be used.

Hamsters are clean, and the cage will have little odor if it receives good ventilation and if the bedding material is changed weekly. The cage should not be placed in a drafty spot, however. Hamsters do best at temperatures in a range of 55° to 80°F (13°–27°C).

If the environmental temperature falls below 48°F (9°C), your hamster will go into hibernation. In hibernation all body functions slow down and the hamster appears to be dead. It will usually revive when the temperature comes back up, but it is best not to allow it to get that cold.

Neither should the cage be placed in direct sunlight where your hamster will get too hot. Put the cage where it will get some sunshine each day. Your pet will enjoy the warmth of the sun, provided it can get into a cool shaded spot when it wants to.

Hamsters are usually kept in separate cages. Mature males almost always will fight even if they have been raised together, and males and females placed together frequently fight. Hamsters don't seem to mind living alone, particularly if you give them frequent attention and if their cage is large enough for them to exercise.

An exercise wheel is part of the equipment each cage should

Commercial cage litter is made of ground corncobs or shredded cane stalks.

have. Hamsters are most active at night, since they are nocturnal. They will run on the wheel for an hour or more at different times during the night. The wheel gives them healthful activity that helps keep them content.

Provide several hardwood limbs about two inches (4–5 cm) in diameter and at least as long as the cage for climbing and chewing. The hamster will do more chewing than climbing, but will enjoy playing on the limbs. Cardboard tubes from inside paper towel rolls placed in the cage will be tunnels for it to play in until the cardboard is chewed up. Small wooden or plastic boxes placed around the cage provide places for storing food, hiding, napping, and play. Don't clutter the cage completely, but do provide a change of furniture arrangement sometimes.

A bored hamster is not a happy hamster. It will just sit in one corner of the cage and droop. It won't have a good appetite, nor will it have the bright alert eyes and shiny coat of a healthy

A healthy hamster has bright, alert eyes and a shiny coat.

hamster. The bored hamster will frequently spend its active period at night throwing the litter in its cage outside, if it can get it through the mesh of the cage sides. It is easy to fix the cage in a manner that will give your pet adequate exercise and make it happy and content. To do less is not fair to this little animal that depends upon you.

You are also responsible for keeping your pet clean. Discard the litter in the cage once a week and replace it with fresh material.

Lack of adequate ventilation is the primary problem with the expensive multilevel plastic cages found in pet supply centers. The solid walls and tops do not provide enough area for ventilation. Most of the creatures in these cages do have some odor and, unless their bedding is changed frequently, the cages are damp.

With a minimum of time and effort and a little help from someone who has some experience in working with hand tools, you can build a suitable cage that will be a hamster palace.

Feeding

There are adequate hamster diets and rodent diets available wherever pet supplies are sold. Rabbit pellets are not a satisfactory diet. If you purchase a prepared diet, be sure it is fresh. When you open the package, the food pellets should be bright and clean, and they should have a fresh food odor and not smell moldy or musty.

Place these food pellets in the cage in a feeding dish that is not easily tipped over. A lid of the size and type used on mayonnaise jars works fine. While fresh pellets provide all the essential food elements your pet is known to require, it will welcome fresh fruit, vegetables, or other treats each day. In fact, a steady diet of dry pellets without occasional fresh foods will often cause bloating and serious digestive upsets.

You need not purchase a prepared food. You can select and feed your hamster an adequate diet from foods available in your home. Hamsters do well if they receive daily some grains such as corn, oats, or wheat, along with some dry kibbled dog food and fresh fruit and vegetables. Breakfast cereals or whole wheat bread can be used with the dry dog-food chunks in place of the grain. But there is no substitute for the fresh fruit and vegetables.

Lettuce, celery, cabbage, carrots, peas, beans, corn, broccoli, and any other vegetables you have should be offered. Apples, bananas, oranges, grapes, tomatoes, and other fruits can be fed. Acorns also may be given. Feed only one or two fruits and vegetables each day, depending on what you have available. But over the month, offer a variety of foods. However, all fresh fruits and vegetables remaining after ten or twelve hours should be removed before they spoil and before the hamster stashes them in its storehouse. Excess dry foods can be stored, but fresh fruit placed in its store pile will cause the whole pile to mold and spoil.

An adult hamster will eat about half an ounce (15 grams) of food per day. Because hamsters pack extra food into their cheek pouches and carry it to their storehouse, most of them do not overeat.

There can be a problem if you feed sunflower seeds. Hamsters love them. And if they are fed an abundance of sunflower seeds, they will become fat. In fact, some hamsters are so fond of them, they will eat only sunflower seeds instead of the other foods they need to balance their diets. For this reason I do not recommend feeding sunflower seeds as part of the basic diet. A few may be given as a treat once in a while, but avoid them as part of the basic diet.

Baby hamsters should be offered fresh vegetables and fruits even while they are still nursing. In fact, when they are ten to sixteen days old and begin eating solid foods, such as dry dog food or hamster pellets, they must have fresh green foods, for dry foods accumulate in a baby hamster's intestine giving it a swollen, bloated appearance. Unless this bloating is relieved, the baby will die. Spinach, celery, lettuce, and other fresh foods will usually relieve bloating or prevent it from occurring.

Nursing babies, as well as adults, should have access to water at all times. The gravity-flow sipper bottle works fine for both. When you have babies, be sure you place the water bottle low enough on the side of the cage for the baby to reach the sipper tube.

Breeding

The hamster is noted for its remarkable ability to reproduce. A young female is mature enough to breed at six or eight weeks of age. She has the shortest known gestation period of any mammal—sixteen days—and may have up to seventeen babies in a litter. It has been estimated that a pair breeding at will, whose young would also be allowed to breed when ready, would be responsible for producing 100,000 individuals within a year's time. You can be overwhelmed with babies.

If you decide that you wish to raise hamsters a few basic rules must be followed. Females are bred at seven or eight weeks of age. You can tell a mature female from the male just by looking at it in the cage. The tiny tail end of a female protrudes beyond the end of its round body. The male has a more pointed tail end and the tail lies in a groove on the two testicles, rather than standing out from the body.

A female is receptive to breeding every four days. If she is placed in the male's cage, she will breed almost at once if it is the correct time in that four-day cycle. If it is not the correct time, they will fight. In this case, the female should be removed and placed in her own cage.

The screened side of her cage should be placed against the male's cage. That way the two hamsters can get used to each other. The following day she may once again be placed in the male's cage. If they do not fight, leave her there for a week and then place her in her own cage. If they do fight, try again the next day. Usually a male and female will adapt to each other and can be kept together for a while. But the female should be separate during the last part of her pregnancy and until the babies are weaned.

The female should have a wooden nest box in her cage. This

simple nest box need only be a six-inch cube (15 × 15 × 15 cm) with a hole large enough for a pregnant mother to enter. Give her some bits of cloth, paper towels, facial tissues, or any other soft material. She will chew them up and make them into a nest, usually in the nest box. Do not handle her during the last part of her gestation.

Sixteen days after breeding, she will have from one to seventeen babies. The average number in a litter is seven.

Do not try to see the babies, to handle the mother, or even to clean the cage for at least three days. This time is critical. If the mother is frightened or feels the babies are threatened, she will try to hide and protect them by stuffing them into her cheek pouches. The tiny baby, which weighs only about a fifteenth of an ounce (2 grams), frequently will die from this rough handling. A panicky mother will sometimes actually eat the babies. Therefore she must have quiet and no visitors for a few days.

The babies have sharp teeth at birth and begin eating almost at once. They grow rapidly. By the time they are three weeks old, they are eating solid foods well and are ready to be weaned.

To tell whether the weanling is male or female, hold the young hamster upside down in the palm of your hand and note the distance from the anal opening to the genital opening. In the males this distance is longer than in the females. It is difficult to make a judgment about one individual, but by comparing several in a litter the difference becomes apparent.

Unless you have a market for the babies, or have homes for the litter, this is the time to give each a separate cage. Unless you use judgment in your decision on breeding, the fun of having a curious happy pet can be replaced with the chores of caring for many unwanted animals.

Diseases

Constipation: All hamsters must have roughage to eat. On a diet without sufficient roughage, hamsters frequently eat the wood chips or bedding material. This undigestible material causes bloating and a distended abdomen. A hamster fed only dry hamster food may also bloat. Feeding fresh green leafy vegetables will provide roughage, moisture, and lubrication to prevent constipation, bloating, and distended abdomen. Feeding foods such as lettuce and spinach is the treatment for this bloated condition. It will help if the hamster is not too severely distended. Severely bloated or constipated hamsters require veterinary assistance to get them unplugged.

Wet Tail: The cause of this condition is unknown, but many believe it is related to improper feeding, which is also the cause of constipation. The area around the anus becomes wet, red, and raw. Sometimes the hamster has diarrhea, while at other times the droppings appear normal. The hamster loses its appetite, appears droopy, and frequently dies in two to three days. Oral antibiotics such as neomycin and choloramphenicol, which are helpful in treatment, must be prescribed by a veterinarian. Proper diet is essential.

Impacted Cheek Pouches: With full cheek pouches, a hamster looks as if it has the mumps. Swelling is seen along the chin and neck on one or both sides. If the swelling does not go down, it means the hamster can't get the food out—the pouch is impacted. Use a blunt forceps or a moistened cotton swab and gently work the food out of the pouch.

Hibernation: If the cage has been placed in a chilly spot, a hamster who appears dead may only be hibernating. This usually occurs below 48°F (9°C). Put the cage in a warmer place and allow the hamster to warm up gradually.

Loss of Hair, Scaly Skin: This can be due to poor diet, mange, or a skin fungus infection. Give a quarter of a teaspoon (1 cc) of corn oil daily in the food, and feed a variety of fresh foods as listed under feeding. If there is no improvement in one month, have a veterinarian examine your pet to determine if it is mange or a fungus. The treatment is different for each.

Internal Parasites (Worms): Pinworms and tapeworms are fairly common in hamsters. These are not transmitted to humans. Both types of worms are usually diagnosed by microscopic examination of fecal droppings. If droppings are normal in appearance and your hamster appears healthy, worms probably are not a problem. If you see worms in the cage or on your hamster, or are taking your pet to your veterinarian for any reason, take a teaspoonful of the droppings along for microscopic examination. Place them in a plastic vial or baggie. If your pet has worms, the veterinarian will prescribe the specific medicine for that parasite.

Upper Respiratory Disease: A hamster has few natural diseases. But if it is kept in a damp, chilly cage, it frequently comes down with a respiratory infection. It will sneeze, its nose drips, it appears listless and doesn't want to eat.

Give it clean dry bedding, put the cage in a warm place— 75° to 80°F (24°–27°C)—and tempt its appetite with bits of bread or oatmeal soaked in milk.

If it doesn't improve in twenty-four to thirty-six hours, antibiotics may be given. Your veterinarian will prescribe one. I prefer chloramphenicol. We give 5–10 mg twice daily with a medicine dropper.

Antibiotic Toxicity: Some antibiotics are toxic to hamsters. Streptomycin given by injection kills a hamster in an hour. Penicillin causes the hamster to die in three to seven days, because it kills normal beneficial bacteria in the intestinal tract and allows others to grow in their place. This is called a gram-negative bacterial enterotoxemia.

Fracture and Concussion: Fractures seldom occur because hamsters have short stocky legs, but concussions are rather common when a hamster is dropped. Most will recover in a couple of days if they are kept warm and quiet. A pregnant female that is dropped usually will die of internal injuries.

Hamsters are hardy and generally quite healthy. With a minimum of care and a little attention, they make enjoyable pets.

References and Suggested Reading

Deitz, N., L. E. Jurrist, and G. W. Meyerholtz. *Pocket Pet 4 H Series.* (No publ. date given).

Dolensek, Emil P., and Barbara Burn. *A Practical Guide to Impractical Pets.* New York: Viking Press, 1976.

Nutrient Requirements of Laboratory Animals. National Academy of Sciences. Washington, D.C., 1972.

Williams, Christine. *A Practical Guide to Laboratory Animals.* St. Louis: C. V. Mosby Co., 1976.

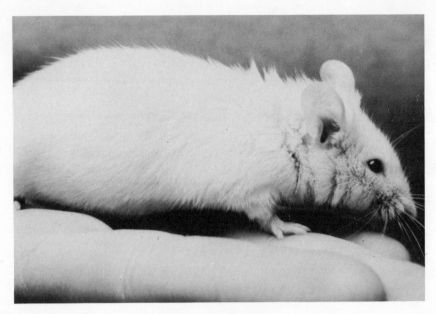

4 / Mice

Mice come in a variety of colors and with a variety of hair coats, but they all look like mice. While there are spotted, black, brown, woolly-coated, angora, and hairless mice, the most popular pet mouse is the plump white mouse.

The average mouse weighs less than an ounce (30 grams), has a hairless tail, sleek body, and rather protruding eyes. Mice are hardy, agile, alert, usually healthy, and if protected from enemies, will live up to three years. Nocturnal creatures, they run, jump, and climb actively most of the night. Although mice will squeak loudly if frightened or hurt, they are relatively quiet. They are nearsighted and timid, but their hearing is well developed as is their sense of smell.

Male mice have a strong "mousy odor," while females do not. For this reason, it is best to choose a female mouse for a pet. Choose an individual that looks bright, alert, sleek, active, and curious. These are signs of health.

Do not start with a pair, for their breeding potential will overwhelm you with babies. It is far better to have one mouse as a pet, then later, if you have found a market and wish to raise mice, buy a male.

Domesticated mice generally make better pets than wild mice. Domesticated mice are easier to tame and less aggressive than wild ones. Wild mice learn to tolerate cages and people. But they don't usually like to be handled and will escape if given the opportunity.

Wild mice may be captured in box traps that will not hurt them. Only by capture and observation can we learn about the species. Wild mice will never be as tame as domestic mice. Nevertheless they are attractive and exceptionally alert. They are fun to observe and to study in order to learn more about their normal behavior and life history.

A small box trap can be used to catch a tame mouse that gets loose, or a wild mouse for study.

Golden mouse, a native wild mouse of Florida.

White-footed mouse. Grasshopper mouse.

Handling

A young mouse, just weaned, is the most easily tamed. Usually it can be picked up by cupping your hand over it and sliding your fingers under its body. If it is not clutched too tightly it usually won't bite, but may bite if it becomes frightened. (If a rodent bite breaks the skin, the scratch should be cleaned with soap and water and treated as any other scrape or wound.)

A young mouse is timid. Once you have it at home in its own cage, it will not take long to make it gentle and friendly. Talk to it while you are around the cage and offer it choice tidbits of food from your fingertips. After a day or so, when it has adjusted to its new home, place your hand—palm up—on the floor of the cage. Most mice explore anything new put in the cage, and your pet will probably come immediately to investigate your hand and crawl up on your palm. When it does, lift your hand slowly out of the cage. Your mouse will crawl over your hand. When it has explored that thoroughly, it will start up your arm. If you place your other hand in its path, it will climb up on that hand. By placing a hand in its line of travel, you can keep it on one hand or the other.

When the mouse becomes used to your hands, let it go on up your arm. It may crawl about on your shoulders, and then, if it acts as most do, it will find a comfortable warm spot and sit down and contentedly groom itself.

If the mouse crawls off or falls off to the floor, it can usually be captured easily. Have a cardboard box about the size of a shoe box ready for such an emergency. Place the box ahead of the mouse with the open end facing the mouse. Gently, using both hands, herd the mouse into the box, tip the box up, and carry the escapee back to its cage.

Later in the day, or the next day, have another taming session. In a few days, if your mouse climbs or falls, place your hand on the floor—palm up—just in front of your friend. It will probably climb back on your hand, for now it has learned to look to you for friendship, attention, and food.

If you obtain an older mouse, follow the same procedure but expect the taming to take longer. If you have patience, even an older mouse that has never been handled will become very tame.

If you must move a mouse, pick it up by its tail. With your thumb and first finger, grasp the tail close to the body. Do not grasp the tip of the tail. If the mouse struggles, the skin may tear and the entire tail covering may come off. Move quickly. As soon as you have hold of the tail, lift the mouse. Do not hold it in a head-down position for more than a couple of seconds. The mouse doesn't like being handled this way and will turn, crawl up its own tail, and bite you.

Move the mouse to where you want it and turn it loose. Or place it on your other hand and release the tail. Unless it is wild and frightened, it won't jump. You can control it by keeping it walking from one hand to the other.

If the mouse must be restrained for some reason, grasp a fold of the loose skin over the neck and shoulders just tight enough to keep the mouse from turning its head back and biting your

A mouse does not like to be handled this way.

fingers. There seldom is any reason for a pet mouse to be handled this way.

Gentleness is slower, but in the long run a much better way to get your pet to accept handling. Reward your mouse with a bit of food when it comes to you. Place a tidbit on your hand to encourage it to climb on the hand. The more attention you give your mouse, the more responsive it becomes. A mouse is naturally shy and timid. When you gain its confidence, you must keep this confidence by talking to it and handling it each day.

Housing

Mice in a laboratory are kept in wire cages six by twelve by six inches (15 × 30 × 15 cm) high. This meets the minimum requirements for a pair of mice. However, it is much nicer if you can provide two or three times this much space for your mouse. Our mice have been most content and healthy in large cages.

The best size is a two-foot cube (60 × 60 × 60 cm). In a cage of this size there is room enough for an area for feeding, a spot for elimination, a nest box, a waterer, and materials for exercise and play.

Everything a mouse needs for a good home: cage, nest box, nest material, brick for·feeding place, waterer, and exercise wheel.

Try building your own mouse cage. Use a piece of exterior plywood for the bottom and for sides that extend up six inches (15 cm) from the bottom. Use half-inch-mesh hardware-cloth to finish off the side walls.

The solid walls at the bottom will keep the absorbent litter in the cage. We usually put two inches (5 cm) of sand or soil, then leaves, wood chips, ground corncobs, sawdust, hay, or any other material available. Newspaper is not recommended, for printer's ink on the paper may make mice sick. A mouse will dig in whatever litter you provide, and unless there are solid sides, the litter is kicked out of the cage and spread everywhere.

Hardware-cloth comes in a twenty-four-inch-wide roll which you bend to conform to the solid sections at the base. The properly bent strip of hardware-cloth is slipped inside the wooden base, making all four walls from one piece of material. Where the ends meet at one corner, wire the hardware-cloth shut. The wood gives the hardware-cloth sides more support; little nailing is needed to fasten the cloth to the wood. The metal walls also protect the wood from the mouse's gnawing teeth.

Cut another piece of hardware-cloth to make the top, and wire it firmly in place. Cut a twelve-inch-square opening (30 × 30 cm) in one side wall to make a door. The door itself can be made of wood or of a folded double thickness of hardware-cloth fastened to the cage with wire. One or more hooks, obtained at the hardware store, securely fasten the door. (See Chapter 13 for details on construction.)

A layer of soil in the bottom of the cage makes the cage easier to take care of. The litter can be removed as required. A mouse usually chooses one specific spot in the cage where it urinates and defecates. Place a disposable aluminum pie plate or tray filled with sand or dirt at this spot. Empty the tray each week, add clean soil, and return the tray to the same spot. The balance of the absorbent litter in the cage seldom needs to be changed.

As has been stated, there is no odor problem when the mouse is a female. But the odor of the male mouse is present to some degree no matter how often the litter is changed.

Each mouse should have an exercise wheel. A wheel provides

needed exercise and prevents boredom. A spinning wheel in the evening is the announcement that this nocturnal rodent is up and starting its day. While you can wake a mouse up during the day and it will welcome your attention, as soon as you leave it will go back to sleep. But at night it will be bustling about. It does need space and equipment to keep it occupied.

Place six or eight sticks of varying lengths and diameters in the cage. Brace the branches against the top and side walls of the cage to form a jungle gym that the mouse can climb and play on. The sticks also provide chewing exercise. Mice, like all rodents, must chew to keep the teeth properly worn down. These hardwood sticks are excellent for the purpose. Replace the sticks when they are badly worn.

Provide a wooden nest box with a mouse-size entrance hole. A mouse will collect bits of paper, cloth, facial tissues, or whatever you make available to make its nest in the box. It needs this retreat to hide in if it is frightened, and to sleep in during the day. We make ours with removable tops but seldom open them, except for an annual cleaning. A nest box six inches (15 cm) square with a one-inch (2.5 cm) entrance hole is fine.

If the mouse is sleeping and you want it to come out and play, a couple of gentle taps on the side or roof of the nest box with a fingertip will bring this curious creature out to see who is knocking on its house.

For added enjoyment, we place cardboard cylinders and aluminum tubing in the cage for tunnels, a couple of bricks stacked for a cave, and anything else we find that looks as if a mouse would enjoy having it to play on.

Since the mouse will be caged 99 percent of its life, the least we can do is make the cage pleasant. Shoebox-size cages, aquariums, and other make-do cages are fine for a short period of time, but are not satisfactory for the lifetime of your pet.

Remember, too, the cage represents food, security, and sanctuary to your mouse. In fact, at our house, if a mouse gets loose we leave its cage door open, and the next morning it will usually be in its nest box sleeping soundly.

Take your mouse out each day and play with it, but then

put it back in its cage. Unlimited freedom to roam the house is dangerous. The mouse can be stepped on, squeezed in a closing door, or eaten by your cat or dog. Your friend is safe in its cage and house.

Feeding

A mouse doesn't eat much and is inexpensive to feed. Although it is active most of the night and nibbles on its food frequently during this time, a mouse will seldom eat more than four or five grams—about a teaspoonful—daily.

Since it eats primarily during the night, it is best to feed your pet late in the evening. Fresh foods will not have a chance to spoil before your mouse eats them.

Mice usually urinate and defecate in the spot farthest from where they are fed. If food is placed in a bowl or dish, some mice will urinate on it after they have eaten their full. This, of course, ruins the food, and it must be discarded. Feeding dishes are not recommended for this reason.

Mice cubes or pellets are available for feeding, but you can also feed foods that you have available. Seeds, bird grain, nuts, bits of brown bread, a piece of dry dog food along with some green vegetables or fresh fruit are the basic diet. Your mouse will relish almost any vegetable, from spinach to turnips. It will also enjoy most fruit and nuts. Offer small portions. A piece of fruit need be only as big as the tip of your finger. Nuts, such as acorns, which you can gather in the fall and place in the freezer until needed, should be offered in the shell. Chewing the shell off provides needed chewing exercise.

Place the grain and small piece of food that might get lost in the litter on top of the nest box. The mouse will eat what it desires during the night and store any remaining seeds in its nest.

Put fruit and fresh vegetables in the branches or on one of the bricks where the mouse will find it during its playtime.

Work out your own preferred feeding method. The important thing is to offer a variety of foods each day. The food should be fresh and in sufficient quantity so that a little is left over each morning. When you check the cage remove and discard any leftover food that might spoil.

If you feed mouse pellets, which can be purchased at a pet supply store, be certain they smell fresh and clean. Musty, moldy-smelling pellets are old and should not be used. Even when you feed this balanced complete ration, your friend will enjoy a daily treat of fresh fruit, a vegetable, or a nut.

Your mouse must have water available at all times. A sipper bottle works fine. It can be wired to the outside of the cage with the tube passing through the hardware cloth in a convenient spot for the mouse to reach. A mouse will drink only a teaspoonful (5 ml) daily. While it would take a month for the mouth to empty the water bottle, it is a good idea to empty and rinse the bottle and offer fresh water each week.

A minimum amount of food, a small expenditure of time, and a good measure of common sense make the feeding of your pet mouse easy, inexpensive, and nutritionally sound.

Breeding

A male mouse is called a buck; a female is a doe. A doe is mature enough to breed by the time it is about two months old. Since she can have up to seventeen litters a year with an average of five to ten babies in each, unless you have a market for the babies—as has been pointed out—they will soon overwhelm you.

If you are aware of this potential problem and still wish to breed your mouse, there are a few things you should know.

The doe has a reproductive cycle that makes her willing to accept a male about every fourth day. This is called an estrous cycle. The male and the female may be kept in the same cage for breeding, during the gestation (pregnancy) period, and after the babies are born. The male is accepted by the female and he will not harm the babies.

If more than one female is to be kept with the male, each

should have its own nest box. Females get along without fighting, but no more than a single male may be kept in one cage. Males will begin fighting soon after weaning. Each attempts to establish dominance and to drive the rival male from its territory.

The gestation period is nineteen to twenty-one days. Baby mice are tiny, helpless, hairless creatures that weigh about a gram at birth. At birth they have pink skin, but by ten days they have their fur. Their eyes are sealed closed until they are about two weeks old.

Babies should not be handled until the doe brings them out of the nest box. When the babies are eating well, usually at about four weeks of age, they can be weaned.

This is also the time to determine the sex of each youngster in the litter. Lift the baby up by using a fold of the skin over the neck and shoulders. Tip the young mouse up so you can see the underside and inspect the area under the tail. In the male the distance from the anus to the genital opening is longer, and a tiny penis is usually visible on the abdomen between the rear legs. After you inspect several babies you will be able to see the difference.

The female babies may be kept together in a cage, for they get along peacefully unless overcrowded. But males should be placed in separate cages. The males inflict wounds on each other while fighting, and if the defeated individual can't escape from its stronger opponent, it may be killed.

There are few problems in breeding mice, but you may have a big problem in finding homes for all the offspring.

Diseases

Bite Wounds: Bite wounds occur between fighting males or overcrowded females in a single cage. Treat wounds with a small amount of an antibiotic ointment. Since mice constantly groom themselves, excess ointment applied to the skin will be eaten.

Antibiotic Toxicity: Mice are not susceptible to the bacterial enterotoxemia of hamsters and guinea pigs. However, they are sensitive to streptomycin, which does kill if injected.

Respiratory Infection and Pneumonia: The depressed mouse sits in a corner with its fur all ruffled up. Some discharge may be noticed from its nose, and it may make a chattering noise as it breathes.

An antibiotic, such as chloramphenicol or tetracycline, can be given orally. A mouse should receive about 5 mg twice daily for four or five days. A 250 mg capsule of the antibiotic is placed in a cupful of water (240 cc) to replace the water in the sipper bottle. A half teaspoonful (2 cc) of sugar may be added to sweeten the water. A mouse should receive four to five mg of antibiotic daily when using this solution. Medicated water should be given for five days.

Tetracycline and chloramphenicol are prescription drugs and must be obtained from your veterinarian or from a drugstore on his prescription.

Diarrhea: Loose runny bowel material is not normal for a mouse. This condition can be due to improper diet, spoiled food, or internal parasites. Correct the diet if it is faulty. If there is no improvement in twenty-four to forty-eight hours, collect as much of the bowel material as possible in a plastic vial and have your veterinarian examine it with the microscope for the presence of internal parasites. If parasites are the problem, he will prescribe the specific medicine required to help your mouse.

Tumors: An unusual lump or swelling that grows on or in your mouse may be a tumor. Mice are susceptible to tumors, and they are common in middle-aged and older mice. Some can be removed surgically. Many are malignant and have spread extensively by the time they are noticed. For these individuals, euthanasia prevents suffering.

Fur Chewing: This occurs when mice are kept together under crowded conditions. Mice chew the fur off the face of their companions. Separate cages or larger cages are needed.

Mites, Fleas, Lice: These tiny parasites are not common in mice. If you see tiny, insectlike creatures crawling through the mouse's hair or attached to the hair, your mouse should be treated. Apply a rotenone-based flea powder to the mouse's fur weekly.

You may also place a Shell pest strip, which contains the insecticide Vapona, on top of the cage one night each week. Do not leave it there continuously. Nor should it be placed where your mouse can chew it or lick it. The insecticidal vapors from the Shell strip will kill most external parasites quickly. Using the strip is an easy way to control these pests.

Mice are generally hardy, self-sufficient individuals. They have few diseases and require minimal health care. Cleanliness, a proper diet, a cage large enough to provide exercise, and a little daily love and attention will ensure a healthy, contented mouse.

References and Suggested Reading

Dolensek, Emil P., and Barbara Burn. *A Practical Guide to Impractical Pets.* New York: Viking Press, 1976.

Williams, Christine. *Practical Guide to Laboratory Animals.* St. Louis: C. V. Mosby Co., 1976.

5 / Rats

The rat has an unpleasant reputation with most people. Because the wild rat is found almost everywhere, is a destructive nuisance, and can be ferocious, perhaps it deserves this unpleasant reputation. But this should not reflect on a pet rat. The pet rat, or laboratory rat, is a direct descendant of the wild brown rat, *Rattus norvegicus*, and is quite different.

The pet rat has the same sleek, streamlined shape, the same type of hair coat and sparsely haired tail as the wild rat, but its disposition sets it apart. The laboratory rat is usually docile, intelligent and friendly. It seems to enjoy human companionship. The one that makes the gentle pet is the white rat. When a white rat gets out of its cage, it usually does not run and hide. It explores the area and stays with you until it finally returns to the security of its cage and food.

A mature male rat weighs about fourteen ounces (420 grams) and the female ten ounces (300 grams). While a rat weighs ten times as much as a mouse, it eats only three times as much. The rat is more intelligent than the mouse, friendlier, not nearly as timid and shy, less apt to bite, and just as easy to care for.

Choose a young rat for a pet, whether white, brown, black, or hooded. Pick one that has a sleek coat, bright eyes, an alert appearance, and the curiosity to come to see you as you look at the cage.

Some pet rats may live to be four years old, but two or three years is average. With reasonable care, these will be enjoyable years for you and your intelligent, curious pet.

Rats do not normally make any noise. They will, however, scream if they are hurt or very frightened.

Handling

As with all rodents, patience and gentleness are the keys to taming and handling. Young rats will tame more readily than older rats. Sudden movements and loud noises should be avoided while you are handling your rat.

Do not pick up a rat by the tail. An adult rat is heavy. Holding it by the tail is uncomfortable for the rat. As it struggles to get free, the skin of the tail may tear loose, leaving you holding only the piece of skin that once covered the poor rat's tail.

A rat is normally picked up by placing one hand around its chest. Slip your thumb in front of one foreleg and under the rat's chin as you slide the first finger in front of the other foreleg. Place the other fingers around the chest and abdomen. If the rat wiggles, do not increase your grip. This will only make the rat struggle more as it gasps for air.

Lift and carry your rat with a secure, gentle grip around the forequarters. However, with a tame rat it is easier to allow it to walk about on your hands and arms as you play with it than to confine it in your hand.

Laboratory rats, which are the ancestors of all pet rats, are not as agile as wild rats or mice. If a rat wiggles loose and falls, it is apt to hurt itself. Concussion and broken legs are common in rats that have fallen from the height of a table or counter.

Talk to your rat, and let it get to know your voice and you. Offer tidbits of food to it in your fingers; this is the quickest way to tame it. Soon it will come to you whenever you come near the cage.

Scientists have found that rats that have been petted and given affectionate attention grow faster, are more alert and active, learn more rapidly, and are better able to withstand stress than rats that are ignored and not petted. When kept as pets, white rats need affection and petting to compensate for the fact that they don't have the company of their own kind.

Housing

A rat becomes quite attached to its cage. It is its home. Build your pet a home of adequate size as soon as you can, and let it

A rat needs an adequate-sized cage, a nest box home, a waterer, and a couple of bricks for a feeding platform.

keep that cage. If you have other rats, don't shift them from cage to cage. Let each have its own. If you sell your rat, give the new owner the home your pet is used to.

Rats need a rather large cage which will provide room for exercise and for the furnishings that you should provide. The two foot-cube cage (60 × 60 × 60 cm) for a mouse (see p. 206) is satisfactory. Make it exactly the same way.

Hardware-cloth also comes in thirty- and thirty-six-inch-width rolls. If you have room for a larger cage, make the bottom thirty or thirty-six inches square and use one of these larger sizes. This would be even better for your pet.

Rats will chew up a wooden cage, so construct your cage using the hardware-cloth to cover as much of the wood as possible. Rats are strong, so your seams and the door must be securely fastened.

The cage should have two to three inches (5–8 cm) of absorbent material in the bottom. You may use wood chips, cat litter, grass clippings, leaves, ground corncobs, or any other material you have on hand. Shredded newspaper is not recommended. The ink comes off on the rat's coat. Since a rat grooms itself constantly, it will lick the printer's ink on its coat and the ink may make it sick. Other types of unprinted shredded paper work fine.

Completely remove and replace all the bedding material in the bottom of the cage each week. This will give you a clean-smelling cage and rat at all times.

Give your rat an exercise wheel. This will provide it with both fun and needed exercise. Branches should be placed in the cage to make a jungle gym for your pet to play on and to provide chewing exercise for its teeth. An old beef bone will also provide chewing exercise, and your pet will enjoy working on it. Fix a shelf high in one corner, a swing to play on, and any other objects you can think of that will make the cage more interesting to your pet.

Place a wooden nest box in one corner of the cage. It should be large enough for your pet to stretch out in and have room enough to turn around. Six inches (15 cm) for each dimension

White rat peers out of her nest box home.

inside is a generous size. A rat-sized hole near the top, which the rat cannot accidentally block when packing down nesting material, will give your pet an entrance. Rats that have branches for chewing exercise will seldom chew up a nest box.

It takes just a little imagination to construct and furnish a cage that will be home for your happy, contented, friendly rodent.

Feeding

Feed your rat once a day. It is not difficult to feed it properly. Complete diets in pellet form are available at most pet supply stores. Although the pellet provides all required nutrients for a basic diet, your pet will appreciate a daily treat of fresh fruit, a vegetable, or some nuts.

It is not necessary however to purchase a special diet for your rat. Dry dog-food chunks can serve as the basis of its diet. In addition to that, feed a variety of other foods, such as carrots, potatoes, apples, spinach, lettuce, corn, tomatoes, whole wheat bread, bird grain, and nuts.

An adult rat will eat a half to two-thirds of an ounce (15–20 grams) of dry dog food each day. The food may be placed in a shallow dish feeder, or it can just be placed on the top of the nest box or on any other clean spot where your rat will find it. The other foods offered can be placed where it is convenient for you and the rat. Any remaining fresh foods should be removed each day when you add additional fresh foods. Don't let food become rotten and spoil.

It isn't necessary to feed all of the supplemental foods each day in addition to the dry dog food. But do offer two or three different foods for variety and as treats. Offer what you have available over a month's time, but try to see that a variety is offered.

When you offer a nut, which is an excellent food and which rats enjoy very much, leave the nut in the shell. The chewing the rat does to open and get at the meat inside is beneficial. It provides the chewing exercise needed to help keep the ever growing teeth worn down.

A gravity sipper water bottle is a fine way to provide water

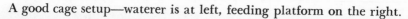

A good cage setup—waterer is at left, feeding platform on the right.

for your rat. It will drink up to two ounces (60 ml) daily. The water bottle should be replenished as needed, and cleaned and rinsed thoroughly each week.

Sometimes medication is given to a rat by mixing it into the water. This is a dependable way to give medication if the rat drinks its usual amount of water. To be sure any bitter taste of the medicine is masked, and because all rats like sweets, add a teaspoonful of sugar to each pint of medicated water. That way it will tempt your pet to drink and ensure that it gets its medication.

Providing fresh water and simple foods is all that is required to see that your rat is properly nourished. Watching your curious pet inspect each item of food you offer each day and then seeing it select the tidbit it likes best, grasp it in both front paws, sit up, and eat with gusto is all a part of the fun of having a pet.

Breeding

If you decide to breed rats, do it while the female is young. Older females bred for the first time don't make good mothers. Females will be mature enough to breed at forty to sixty days, but you should wait until they are sixty to ninety days old.

The females are willing to breed all seasons of the year. Female rats have an estrous cycle that makes them willing to accept the male and breed about every five days. A male and female may be placed together in a cage.

Females ovulate at the time of breeding, and the babies are born in twenty-one to twenty-two days from that time. The hairless, helpless babies weigh about a sixth of an ounce (5 to 6 grams) at birth. While the average number is nine, there may be up to fourteen in the litter. The male will not harm the babies.

A mother rat is a good mother. She will hover protectively over her nest, lavish affection on her brood, and retrieve any babies that crawl or fall out of the nest. The female will allow the male into the nest area, and he will help clean and care for the babies.

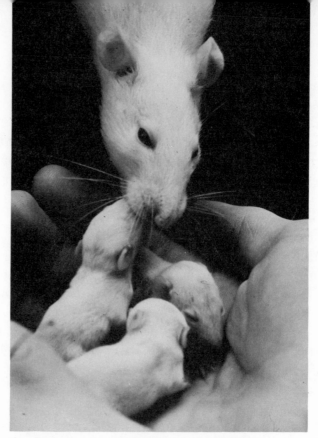

A mother rat "rescuing" one of her babies.

The babies' eyes open when they are fourteen to fifteen days old. They grow rapidly, learn to eat solid food quickly, and are ready to be weaned when they are three weeks old.

You can tell the difference between the male and female babies by comparing the distance between the anal and genital openings. In the male this distance will be twice that in the female. Males and females should be separated to prevent young females from being bred before they are mature. Males must be separated if they start fighting with each other.

Only one female of breeding age should be in the cage with a male. A female that has young is protective and will attack another female who comes near the nest.

If you wish only one litter, remove the male as soon as the babies are born or before. Females will breed and conceive within a day or so after the babies are born.

Unless you can sell the babies or give them away, you are

better off not breeding your rat. Having dozens of rats is a lot of work. They require cages, food, and so much time in routine care that there seldom is any time left for affection or attention to individual rats. One rat, given some time and attention, can be a gentle, curious pet that will return all the attention and affection you give.

Diseases

Keep your pet rat where it will not come in contact with wild rats. Wild rats have fleas, ticks, and other pests. They also can carry diseases that are contagious to your rat and, in some cases, even to you.

Red Tears: There are glands in the eyelids that secrete a pigmented material (porphyrins) mixed with tears. When this material dries on the lids or around the nose, it looks like a crust of blood. Such material is most noticeable in white rats and becomes more pronounced as your rat gets older. There is no cause for worry and these red tears require no treatment.

Bulging Eyeballs (Sialodacryo-adenitis): This condition is caused by a virus that invades the salivary glands. The salivary glands produce saliva and are located just under the skin under the chin and around the ears and eyes. Swelling of these glands causes swollen cheeks and bulging eyeballs. The eyes may be pushed outward so far that the eyelids can't close.

There is no specific treatment. Protect the eyeballs from drying out by applying one drop of castor oil to each eye several times a day.

In ten to fourteen days the swelling will go down, and the rat will return to its normal appearance.

Small Eyes (Microopthalmia): If a diet deficient in vitamin A has been fed to a female over a period of time, baby rats will not develop normal-sized eyeballs. There is no treatment to help these individuals. Feeding a proper diet with foods rich in vitamin A will prevent the occurrence of this condition in the next litter.

Tumors: A swelling or growth can occur anywhere in the rat's body. As in people, if tumors are detected early and removed surgically, the individual has a good chance for recovery.

Fleas and Lice: These parasites are not seen frequently. If they are found on your pet, dust it with a cat flea powder weekly for three to four weeks.

Internal Parasites (Worms): Pinworms—not the same pinworms that affect humans—are common in rats. They do not cause a problem in most rats. However, collect a teaspoonful of *fresh* bowel droppings, place it in a plastic vial, and take it to a veterinary hospital for microscopic examination.

If your pet has internal parasites, your veterinarian will prescribe the specific medicine for that parasite. For example, tapeworms are a form of internal parasite. Rats can have two different kinds of tapeworms. While it is not common, both are capable of infecting humans. The rat with tapeworms is treated with Niclosamide at the rate of 50 mg per pound (100 mg per kilogram) of body weight daily for one week. This drug is mixed into the food offered each day.

Pneumonia and Chronic Respiratory Disease: These are two similar conditions in rats caused by bacterial organisms. An affected rat is depressed, has a discharge from the nose, coughs, sneezes, and doesn't eat well.

Antibiotics help in this condition. Dissolve two 250 mg capsules of tetracycline or chloramphenicol—both prescription drugs—in a pint of water. Add a teaspoon of sugar to mask the somewhat bitter taste. Usually this will provide a therapeutic amount of the antibiotic when given by the sipper bottle for five days.

Rats do not develop enterotoxemia—antibiotic toxicity—as do guinea pigs and hamsters.

Rats have made an important contribution to the health of man. Used as models in the laboratory, they have helped us learn to control such diseases as polio and tuberculosis. Fortunately, rats themselves are hardy and seldom need specific health care. But they do need a daily amount of love and attention to stay healthy.

References and Suggested Reading

Dolensek, Emil P., and Barbara Burn. *A Practical Guide to Impractical Pets*. New York: Viking Press, 1976.

Williams, Christine. *Practical Guide to Laboratory Animals*. St. Louis: C. V. Mosby Co., 1976.

6 / Gerbils

The gerbil is a popular pet for several reasons. While most other rodents are primarily nocturnal, the gerbil is active during the day. It has a gentle disposition, a natural curiosity, and no fear of people. It seldom makes more noise than an occasional *cheep* and if it gets loose, it doesn't try to hide.

Gerbils look somewhat like small rats. They weigh two to four ounces (60–120 grams) and have the same general shape as rats, but their tails have hair in contrast to the bare tail of the rat. They are called desert rats by some, but their proper name is *Meriones unguiculatus*.

Originally they came from the desert area of Mongolia in the northernmost area of China. The first gerbils were imported in 1954. As desert animals they avoided the greatest heat of the day by going deep in the burrows they dig. Their bodies have adapted to desert life by requiring little water. They therefore secrete very little urine. And their sandy-brown color, which blends into the desert terrain, helps them avoid enemies and predators.

Although gerbils are not nocturnal, they are active at night as well as during the day. A gerbil's twenty-four-hour day is made up of periods of intense activity punctuated by long naps.

Popular as pets and laboratory animals, gerbils are hardy, breed rapidly, and live for two to four years. Because they do breed rapidly and are able to survive so well in the desert, they are banned from several western states. They could become serious pests if a pair were released.

These clean, attractive, inquisitive, intelligent desert rodents are the choice of more and more people as pets.

Handling

With gentle handling a gerbil quickly becomes a friend. If you handle gerbils roughly or if they become frightened, they will bite.

Tempt the little creature to become acquainted with you by offering tidbits of food from your fingers. When the gerbil has learned to come looking for food and to greet you, you can place the tidbit on the palm of your hand and put your hand in the cage. The inquisitive gerbil will usually climb on your hand and begin eating.

When the gerbil is on your hand, you can lift it up and out of the cage. Be careful; don't let it fall. Gerbils have little fear of height and will walk off your hand. A fall to the floor may injure it. Use your other hand to keep your gerbil from falling —place it so it acts as a protective barricade.

If you sit down on the floor and place your hand in your lap, the gerbil will crawl about on your legs and hand exploring. Your hand can be used as a barricade to keep your pet from wandering.

If your gerbil gets away from you and manages to get down on the floor, it will usually stay close to you. You can recapture it by placing a tidbit of food on the palm of your hand and allowing the gerbil to crawl up on your hand. If this doesn't

Place your hand so that it acts as a protective barricade.

Cover the open end of the can with your palm and transport the gerbil back to its cage.

work, place an empty tin can with a choice bit of food in it on the floor near your pet. The gerbil will enter the can. You can then place your hand over the open end, lift the can up, and transport your friend back to its cage.

As a rule, your gerbil should not be picked up by the tail. In an emergency, however, this method of handling may be used. Grasp your gerbil at the base of its tail with one hand to hold it still. Then with the other hand quickly grasp the loose skin over the shoulders to lift it. This is effective, but most gerbils resent it. Handling your pet this way will not help make it tame.

Once your gerbil knows you as a friend, it will look forward to the time you spend with it. It will allow you to scoop it up in your cupped hand and then grasp it around the chest and abdomen to lift it. It will allow you to handle it almost any way as long as you talk to it softly and handle it gently.

Housing

More than one gerbil may be kept in a cage. If a group has been together since weaning, they will usually not fight. Even two males will live together peacefully if they are placed together as youngsters. However, if you keep a group of males and females together in a cage, you can expect to be overwhelmed by babies. Also, overcrowding will cause fighting.

Putting two adult males together will cause a fight. If the weaker individual can't escape, it may be killed. Adding a strange gerbil to a group will also cause a battle. Unless you are going to breed gerbils, the best practice is to keep one individual in each cage.

The cage should be constructed of hardware-cloth with a wooden base as shown in Chapter 13. The two-foot-square cage described there is an ideal size for a single pet. Gerbils love to gnaw, so exposed wooden portions of the cage must be protected with hardware-cloth or some other metal.

Gerbils also love to dig in the litter in the cage. They will spend hours digging and rearranging the absorbent material in the bottom of the cage. Unless the cage has solid sides six to eight inches (15–20 cm) up from the base, the litter will be scattered all around the outside of the cage.

Smaller cages, aquariums, plastic pet-shop cages can also be used, but a cage large enough to allow room for toys and exercise, with open sides that give good ventilation, is the most desirable.

Gerbils do best if they are in a dry environment. A damp cage makes their hair coat appear matted and rough. A damp, humid cage causes skin problems and makes this desert rodent much more susceptible to respiratory infections. A humidity of 50 percent is ideal, with temperatures from 50° to 80°F (10°–27°C). However, the gerbil is adaptable and will get along in less than an ideal environment.

Use deep absorbent bedding in your cage. Three to four inches (8–10 cm) is fine. Wood chips, leaves, sand and soil, burlap sacking, shredded newspapers, ground corncobs, sawdust, or other materials may be used. Fun time for your gerbil is digging and making tunnels and caves in this material, so be sure it is deep enough.

Since gerbils do not excrete much urine, it is usually not

A large aquarium can serve as a rodent cage.

necessary to change the litter each week. If you have just one gerbil in the cage, with plenty of litter, the cage seldom needs changing more than once a month. In fact, we usually don't change the cage until we detect an odor from it. If the cage looks and smells clean we leave it be.

Place a couple of empty tin cans in the cage for caves and burrows. One or two pieces of one-inch (2.5 cm) metal tubing or pipe make good tunnels for playtime. Several hardwood branches should be placed in the cage and arranged for climbing. Although gerbils don't do as much climbing as other rodents, they enjoy chewing on the branches. This helps keep their teeth worn down.

An exercise wheel should be placed in the cage. It may be suspended from the top of the cage with wires or placed on a wooden base on a low shelf. More often than not, you may find the exercise wheel partially buried in a pile of litter or tipped over as the gerbil excavates under it in its normal digging. Some gerbils never seem to use a wheel, others enjoy it. But all gerbils get adequate exercise digging and shifting the litter about their cage.

A nest box may be placed in the cage. But if a couple of different-sized tin cans are provided, your gerbil will usually make its home in one of these. It will shred soft bits of the litter and collect it for the nest. The entrance into the can will be from a tunnel under the bedding material.

We place a couple of bricks on top of each other against one side of the cage as a food platform. The gerbil can't move the bricks about, and two bricks on top of each other make a clean platform above the level of the litter. You can place the food on this clean, stable platform.

A water bottle can be wired to the side of the cage. The spout

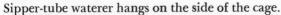

Sipper-tube waterer hangs on the side of the cage.

should be high enough so that it doesn't contact the litter as it is shifted about, but low enough for your pet to reach it. Place it on the side of the cage above the brick feeding platform. It will be protected from the litter but convenient for your pet.

Gerbils are the cleanest and least smelly of all the rodents that are kept as pets. They require little equipment and less care than most caged pets. With their quiet, gentle disposition and affectionate, inquisitive temperament, it is easy to see why gerbils are popular as pets.

Feeding

Laboratory animal rodent pellets provide a complete diet for gerbils. They will eat a third to a half ounce (10–15 grams) daily. The pellets can be obtained from a pet supply store. A complete diet of this type requires no supplemental feeding. However, if you feed pellets, your gerbil will enjoy a little fruit, nuts, or vegetables each day as a treat.

It is not necessary to purchase a special diet if you use a little judgment in feeding. Offer a few pieces of dry dog or cat food as the constant basic part of the diet. Then each day give additional foods as supplements and to provide variety. Your gerbil should have fresh fruits and vegetables every day. Brown bread bits, breakfast cereals, bird grain, a piece of carrot, potato, or apple, a small leaf of lettuce, cabbage, or celery, and green peas, raisins, lima beans, or nuts can be offered. Your gerbil will enjoy and do well on a diet of this type. Normally it will eat about a tablespoonful (15 grams) of food each day. Extra seeds will be stored in a cache under the litter.

Gerbils, like all rodents, love sunflower seeds. They will eat them exclusively if given the chance. This is not good, for they won't be eating the foods they should eat. A diet primarily of sunflower seeds leads to nutritional deficiency. Poor skin and hair coat, fragile bones, and a droopy gerbil will be the end result of this diet. An occasional sunflower seed as a treat is fine, but don't make them a major part of the diet.

It is true that in its natural habitat the gerbil gets along on very little water. This does not mean that while it is in your care it should be deprived of water. A sipper tube and water bottle should always be available. Some gerbils won't drink much, but most will drink as much as other mammals of similar size.

It is important to provide a few hardwood branches, nuts in their shells, or a large beef bone for chewing. Without chewing exercise a gerbil's incisor teeth will grow out until it is no longer able to eat properly. Frequently, a thin undernourished gerbil is the result not of improper food or not enough food, but of the gerbil's being unable to chew its food. It is easy, yet necessary, to prevent this from happening to your pet.

A gerbil is easy to feed. It will enjoy almost any food you offer. With just a little care in the selection of what you offer, you can be sure your friend will be healthy, content, and well fed.

Breeding

As with most rodents, breeding and having litters of babies is not a problem if you know a few pertinent facts. Disposing of a flood of babies can be a big problem, so don't breed your pet unless you have a home for them.

Females are mature enough to breed when they are ten weeks of age. A mature male and female can be placed together in a cage. Usually they will get along very well. Males may be left with the females even after the babies are born.

Females are receptive to breeding every four to six days year round. Ovulation occurs at the time of breeding, and the babies are born twenty-two to twenty-four days later. The litter will vary from three to twelve small, hairless babies. However, the average litter usually is only about five, each weighing about a tenth of an ounce (2.5–3 grams).

The babies grow fast, for a gerbil mother is a good mother. She feeds and cares for them until they are eating solid food. They are old enough to be weaned at about three weeks.

At this age you can tell male from female babies by examin-

Female gerbil is at left, male at right.

ing the distance from the anal to the genital opening. In males this distance is twice as long as it is in the females. By comparing two or three of the weanling babies, you can readily learn to tell the difference.

Weaning time is the time to sell or give the babies to their new owners. At this age young gerbils are easiest to tame and are most dependent upon the owner for companionship. You, as the breeder, will be regarded as the expert. Explain carefully how to care for and feed this new baby. Be certain that each baby has a home where it will receive not only considerate care, but ample attention and affection.

Diseases

Bald Nose: Usually the loss of hair from the area of the head between the nose and the eyes is due to excessive digging, thrusting its nose through the cage openings, and pushing litter about with the nose.

There is no treatment required except to choose a bedding material that is softer and not as abrasive.

Tail Chewing: A symptom of this appears as loss of hair along the tail. This bad habit most frequently occurs when gerbils are bored or overcrowded. They chew the hair off the tail in random patches. Regard this as an indication that you need to change the way you are keeping you pet. Provide more room for exercise and toys for play.

Patchy loss of hair over the tail and body, where the hair is not lost by chewing, can indicate a fungus infection. If your gerbil has patches of scaly skin visible, have your veterinarian examine it and prescribe the specific medicine required.

Red Tears: A normal secretion from the glands in the eyes appears as a crust of dried blood in the inner corner of the eye or at the nose. This material, called porphyrins, is normal and requires no treatment.

Coprophagy: Eating the pellets eliminated as bowel material is a normal habit in gerbils, rabbits, and some other mammals. It requires no treatment.

Seizures or Convulsions: Convulsions like those of epilepsy may occur in some gerbils. Most frequently they occur during stress, during handling, or when the gerbil is frightened. These seizures may last from three to ten minutes. The cause is unknown, but it appears to be an inherited condition that shows up in certain females.

There is no treatment. Just leave the gerbil quietly alone. Don't handle the gerbil while it is having a seizure, for it may accidentally bite.

Fleas and Lice: These are seldom a problem. Gerbils scratch and groom themselves a great deal. Don't assume they have external parasites because they scratch.

If you actually see small brown fleas or tiny gray lice on their hair or bodies, dust them well with a cat flea powder weekly.

Staphylococcal Infection: In this disease the skin will appear puffy and red. Scabs will form on the damaged skin. This infection sometimes spreads over the feet, tail, and abdomen. It can be fatal to your gerbil.

It is treated with antibiotics. Usually 250 mg of tetracycline or chloramphenicol is dissolved in four ounces (120 ml) of water. Add a quarter of a teaspoonful (1 gram) of sugar to the solution to mask the bitter taste. Use this mixture instead of the drinking water for the next ten days. However, in five days throw out the old solution in the bottle and replace it with a fresh solution.

Respiratory Infection: Coughing, sneezing, and dripping from the nose are signs of a respiratory infection. The infection is usually a staphylococcal or strephtococcal infection. The same mixture used for staphylococcal infections may be used in upper respiratory infections.

Gerbils do not suffer from the antibiotic toxicity and enterotoxemia of hamsters and guinea pigs. The antibiotic streptomycin given by injection will kill gerbils, however.

Gerbils are surprisingly healthy. As a veterinarian, I find most of the problems I see related to either poor care or poor nutrition. Small cages, damp bedding, and inadequate ventilation create an unhealthy environment for your gerbil. Feeding a limited choice of foods or old musty commercial foods also causes problems.

Both of these situations are easy to correct. You know from reading the sections on feeding and housing what is required. A gerbil places minimal demands on you for care, and you owe it to your pet to provide this basic housing and a clean, varied diet.

References and Suggested Reading

Glick, P. R. "What About Gerbils?" in *Modern Veterinary Practice.* February 1970.

Williams, Christine. *Practical Guide to Laboratory Animals.* St. Louis: C. V. Mosby Co., 1976.

7 / Chickens

It used to be popular at Easter to give children baby chicks as a present. Fortunately, this isn't done anymore. Great numbers of such chicks died of neglect and many more from the ignorance of their owners. On the other hand, many young people have lost the chance to become acquainted with them as pets. This is a shame, for chickens enjoy your company and attention, require little work or care, and reward you with fresh, nutritious eggs.

Chickens are divided into two general classes: those that have been bred for their ability to lay eggs are called layers; and those that are plump and tasty, and have been bred to serve as food—called meat chickens. There is a third group that fits in between the two. These are dual purpose breeds. They do not lay as many eggs as a layer, but they are plumper than most layers and are suitable as a meat chicken also. The best known of the layers are white Leghorns, which lay white eggs. The best known dual-purpose chickens are the Rhode Island Red, Plymouth Rock, and Barred Rock, all of which lay brown eggs. Our favorites are the Rhode Island Reds, because they are friendly, have an even disposition, lay a reasonable number of eggs, and are good foragers. Bantam chickens, which are miniature chickens, are not good layers nor good meat chickens, but they do make good pets.

Chickens may be purchased from Sears and Montgomery Ward mail-order catalogs and from ads in many farm and outdoor magazines. They are sold at most feed stores at different times of the year. Regardless of where you purchase your chickens, get them as young as possible. This way you become the mother hen and the chicks are attached to, or imprinted on, you. If they are treated gently while they grow up, they will always be glad to see you even when they are adult layers.

Young chicks are sold as straight-run, which means no effort has been made to distinguish between males and females, or as sexed chicks, which means they have been sorted into pullets (females) and cockerels (males), which grow up to be roosters. Whether you are buying one or ten chicks, by all means choose pullets.

You will be getting chickens that have the potential to lay eggs. With straight-run chicks, you will have to do something with the males. If you can't face killing and eating them, you will discover it is difficult to find a home for them. When you have several roosters, they fight.

We enjoy having one rooster. We like to wake up and hear him crow. It would be neighborly, if you have close neighbors, to make sure they also like to hear your rooster announce the morning's arrival. Sometimes, even a single rooster can be a problem. Some become very belligerent as they get older. They will attack small children, dogs, cats, and even adults. A rooster is a natural bully. Although he will seldom attack the person who raised him, with his sharp claws and spurs he will terrorize all those who have shown themselves to be afraid of him and all those who flee from his attacks. This bullying behavior is another good reason for choosing pullets.

The number of chicks you choose depends on your goals and desires. If you want a dependent pet, choose a single chick. Chickens are social creatures. Your chick will need you to give it companionship and attention. If you want pets who are more independent, who are glad to see you but provide companionship for each other, choose three pullets. The housing required is not much larger, and three will give you a meaningful number of eggs during the year.

Pick out chicks that are active, alert, curious, and have bright, shiny down. Check the down around the vent. This is a polite word for the anal opening. If this area is wet, soiled, or smeared with droppings, exchange the chick for another.

If your chicks come by mail, open the package at the post office or in the presence of the mail carrier. Breeders will replace chicks if the post office personnel certify they were sick or dead on arrival. This doesn't happen often, for breeders are experienced in preparing chicks for shipment and the post office has learned to speed delivery of chicks.

Some feed stores and breeders sell debeaked chicks. Debeaking means that the end of the top beak, or of both top and bottom beaks, has been cut off. This may be an advantage to a commercial poultry farmer, for it keeps the chickens from pecking at each other. It is not a desirable situation for you. The chicks appear mutilated, and when they are adults it is difficult for them to forage and pick up bugs and seed grains.

Plan ahead and have the housing ready for your chicks before they arrive.

Housing

When chicks are tiny you must provide the four basics for their survival: warmth, food, water, and protection from weather and predators.

A cage to provide all of these necessities for three pullets can be easily built or prepared.

A cage with warmth for baby chicks is called a brooder. A brooder two feet wide, two feet long, and one foot high (60 ×

60× 30 cm) is fine. While a large cardboard box can be used, a wooden cage is better. The bottom and at least two of the sides should be of solid material such as exterior plywood. The other two sides can be of half-inch hardware-cloth. The solid sides protect the chicks from drafts. The hardware-cloth sides provide adequate ventilation and allow the chicks to see out. A top should be placed on the brooder to protect the chicks from cats or other predators.

Purchase a porcelain ceiling light fixture from any hardware store to provide warmth. Be sure all exposed wires are covered with electrician's tape, then place the fixture on the floor of the brooder. Fit it with a 60-watt bulb. Place the light near a protected corner where it is sheltered from drafts. Place a thermometer on the floor near the fixture. The temperature should be 95°F (35°C). If it isn't, use a higher watt bulb. The chicks will move in close to the light for warmth when they need it. They will need this extra warmth until they are four to six weeks old.

Cover the bottom of the entire cage with papers. Change the papers daily.

If the chicks are to be pets, be sure to hold each chick several times every day. It will enjoy snuggling up in the cupped palms of your hands.

In a brooder where the chicks are protected, they thrive and grow rapidly. During the warm part of the day, remove them from the brooder and take them out on the grass for short periods. The chicks will follow you as you walk about. Talk to them to encourage them, for you are acting as the mother bird now. Sit with them on the grass. They will stay near you and search about for seeds and bugs. If they become tired or cold they will crawl up on your lap, snuggle up to get warm, and take a nap. This is the signal to take them back to the brooder.

By acquainting them with the world outdoors, you are teaching them to follow you, to find their way around your yard, and to find food. These outdoor sessions need not be long, but should take place every day.

When the chicks have feathers over most of their bodies, they can be left outside alone during the day. Take their brooder out on the grass. Take the top off and tip the brooder on its side, so the chicks can get in and out through the top opening. Run an extension cord to their light so they can have warmth when they want it, and be sure they have food and water.

The young chickens will explore around the brooder. They will scratch, eat, and chase one another around. When they are tired or hungry, they will return to the brooder and nap. They will run to greet you when you come to see them and will be ready to be brought in long before the evening chill sets in.

As they get older, allow them to spend most of the day out of doors. If they are not going to be allowed to roam free, this is the time to construct a fenced yard, for exercise, and a small chicken house. Unless it is very cold outside, they will no longer need the warmth of their brooder light.

The chicken house, or coop, is a sanctuary for nighttime protection, to protect your chickens from weather and predators. If the weather is reasonably warm, your chickens can begin to spend nights in the coop when they are six to eight weeks old.

A chicken coop need not be large. Provide three square feet (2700 square cm) of floor space for each bird. Give more space if you can, for later you may decide to add more pullets to your group. We place a welded wire floor about twelve to eighteen inches (30–45 cm) above the ground in our coop. Mesh with openings about a half by one inch (1 $\times$ 2.5 cm) provides secure footing while allowing all the droppings to fall through to the ground below. Two perches, wrist-thick tree branches, are placed twelve to eighteen inches (30–45 cm) above the floor, along the back and side of the coop about six inches (15 cm) from the wall. Chickens sleep, or roost, on these perches at night.

Opposite the perches, we place nest boxes, to give the pullets a secure spot for their eggs when they begin laying. These are wooden boxes one foot (30 cm) square, with an open side facing the central area of the coop. Line the bottom of each nest with a soft nesting material, such as hay or cloth. One nest should be provided for each four pullets. But always have at least two nests. If two of your hens have the urge to lay at the same time, one nest gets crowded.

Each hen has its favorite nest. When it is time for one to lay and she finds another hen in the nest, the complaining hen will voice her displeasure and continue cackling until "her" nest is vacated.

The coop should have a door that can be closed at night to protect the chickens from night-roaming predators. The chickens will go in the coop to roost at dusk. Close the door when they are all in. Confined until morning, they will be safe.

Egg Laying

Eggs are the tangible benefit of having pullets as pets. A pullet will begin laying when it is five or six months of age.

While chickens live for as long as six to ten years, they usually will lay eggs for only about three years. A good laying hen will lay as many as two hundred eggs in a year's time.

Cold weather, along with the shorter days of winter, slows down egg production. Egg laying also stops once a year while the hen molts. Molting is the shedding of old feathers and their replacement by new ones. This feather growth requires all the hen's energies and a molting hen will not lay for six to eight weeks. During the second season of egg laying after her molt, she will not lay as many eggs as she did in her first season. Each year a hen lays fewer eggs.

Some hens never seem to lay well. If you are interested in getting the most eggs from your hens, remove the poor layers from the group. A farmer regards his chickens as an investment. Since he pays for the food they eat, only those that produce eggs and pay their own way remain in the flock. At our house, since the chickens are friends, too, we carry the freeloaders along with the better hens.

You can tell which hens are laying. An active laying hen has a bright red comb and a large moist vent. A nonlaying hen has a dull-colored comb, and the vent will appear small and dry.

Gather your eggs daily and refrigerate them promptly to keep them at their peak of quality.

Laying can be stimulated by increasing the length of the chicken's day. Hens can be pushed for maximum egg production by using the light to make the days fourteen hours long. This makes the hen believe it is summer always, and she won't go into the decreased laying associated with winter.

However, at our house our hens roam free, eat bugs, and find part of their own food, so we don't demand much from them. We don't manipulate the hours of daylight. The eggs we receive are a bonus, for we enjoy just having chickens.

Feeding

Your baby chicks should be fed and given water as soon as you get them. Usually they are shipped without food, for they are born with a built-in supply of food—the yolk of the egg that is being absorbed by their bodies. The supply lasts about three days.

Buy a starting mash from a feed store and have it ready when the chicks arrive. Starter mash is a mixture of ground corn, oats, barley, alfalfa, soybean meal, and other foods. It contains about 20 percent protein and all the vitamins and minerals your baby chicks need.

Place some starter mash in one or more jar lids near the brooder light. Scatter other bits of mash about on a large piece of plain paper (no newsprint) near the light to entice the chicks to start eating. Use a second jar lid to provide water.

If the chicks do not begin eating after they get warmed up, try to teach them. Pick up bits of the mash and drop it in front of a chick. Gently tap the paper with the tip of your finger near a bit of mash. Try to show the chick that the mash is food. This is what a mother chicken does. She picks up bits of food as she clucks, calling the chick to her. Then she drops it in front of the chick. If it doesn't see it and eat it, she repeats the procedure until it gets the idea. This is what you must do, too.

Once one chick learns to eat, the others will learn by imitat-

Baby chicks eating starting mash, with the light bulb for warmth.

ing it. Feed the starting mash for about six weeks, then switch to a growing mash. Chicks are fed growing mash until they start to lay. Food should be available for them to eat at all times.

As the chicks get older you can make a troughlike feeder for them, or buy one at the feed store where you get their mash. A feeder a foot (30 cm) long is big enough for four to six birds.

When your pullets start laying, change to a laying mash. A laying hen will consume one and one-half to two pounds of food per week.

When laying, they also need to have cracked oyster shells. This material, a rich source of calcium, is used in producing the shell of the eggs. Most chickens won't eat a lot of oyster shell, but it should be available.

Chicks, pullets, and laying hens should also have grit in their diet. This is a form of ground granite available at feed stores. Grit comes in different sizes—small for baby chicks, and

A homemade feeder provides laying mash for your chickens.

larger sizes for adults. Offer the grit in a separate feeder. Grit functions as a grinding agent in the gizzard of your chicken. Chickens allowed to roam freely in your yard usually pick up all the grit they need, but since a chicken will eat less than a pound (450 grams) a year, it is good insurance to keep grit available at all times.

All chickens need water. Baby chicks should be given water in a jar lid as soon as you get them. If they don't drink, touch their beaks in it to be sure they learn to drink.

After a few days switch to a waterer that uses an inverted mason jar. These waterers are inexpensive and available at all feed stores. A waterer of this type prevents the chicks from walking through their water and provides a more adequate and dependable supply. Change the water each day and rinse the waterer thoroughly as you do so.

Part of the satisfaction of properly feeding and caring for

Raised with gentleness, these young chickens are pets.

your pullets will be the knowledge that your effort and dollars
spent for feed will be returned in good eggs.

Breeding

In order to have fertile eggs capable of hatching, you must have
a rooster with your hens. All eggs laid are then fertile. They
can be eaten too. Or else, if you want more chicks, the eggs can
be gathered, placed in an incubator, and hatched. If you use an
incubator, follow the recommendations of the manufacturer.

Normally the incubation temperature for chicken eggs is
100°F (37.8°C). Humidity should be at least 60 percent so the
eggs won't dry out. The eggs must be turned at least twice

A quart mason jar is dependable and assures an adequate water supply.

daily. Four or five times per day during the first two weeks is even better. Rotate the egg halfway on each turn. Position the small end of the egg lower than the large end. Chicken eggs hatch after twenty-one days of incubation. If you mark the date on each egg with a pencil when it is placed in the incubator, you will know when it will hatch.

Rather than hatching the eggs in an incubator, it is far easier to let one of your hens hatch and care for the baby chicks for you. Usually at least once a year the nesting urge strikes each hen. You can easily tell, for the hen will stay on the nest day and night. The urge to incubate the eggs is so strong that when you take the eggs that were laid from under her, she will incubate an empty nest. If you lift her out of the nest, she will complain loudly and stalk about clucking grumpily until she can

Rhode Island Red in the nest box laying an egg.

get back in the nest. She may leave the nest long enough to get
a drink of water, but then she will climb back into her nest.
A hen that behaves this way is called broody.

If you want more chicks, let the broody hen keep her eggs
and give her some fertile eggs from the other hens, but she has
finished laying her own.

Some broody hens will not use the nest box, but will hide
their eggs in a nest they fashion themselves. At first the hen will
not spend a great deal of time on this hidden secret nest. She
will lay an egg a day until she has a full "clutch" of ten or so
eggs. Then she will begin to incubate in earnest. She will leave
the nest only for short intervals to get a drink and pick up a
few quick bits of food, but she will spend most of her time
incubating. By waiting to incubate the eggs till she has a clutch

of eggs, she ensures that all the chicks hatch the same day.

When you notice a hen isn't coming to the coop at night, you must find her. When you see her out in the yard feeding, follow her and let her lead you to her nest. If you feel she has chosen a safe spot, and you want chicks, let her stay there.

If it isn't safe from nighttime predators, or you don't want chicks, take the eggs, destroy the nest, and place the broody hen in a small cage. Usually if you confine a broody hen in a small— eighteen-inch-cube (45 × 45 × 45 cm)—cage with food and water for two to three days, the broody spell will be broken. She frequently will start laying again. If she is still broody when you release her, she will start incubating again at her old nest. You will have to repeat this confinement again for three or four days. When the broody spell is over, her behavior will be like the other layers'.

If a hen hatches chicks, you must provide a safe place for mother and babies for several weeks. A mother hen and chicks are no match for a fox, possum, or raccoon. The mother hen keeps her babies warm at night by cuddling them under her feathers. She and they can't roost on the perches in the chicken coop as the other adult chickens do. The chicks can't get up on the roost, and the mother can't keep them warm there.

Provide a separate cage, confine her in a closed shed or garage, or place her in one of the laying nests in the coop and place the babies in with her every evening. They will snuggle under her wings and feathers to spend the night.

If you are going to confine her to the coop at night, place papers or boards over the welded wire floor to keep the babies from falling through as the mother hen leads them outside in the morning.

Regardless of where you decide to keep her and the babies, you should check each night at dusk to be certain the family is secure.

When the chicks begin to feather out at about four weeks of age, mother hen will take them to the coop. At night they will perch or roost as a family on one of the perches.

It is best that hens be allowed to hatch chicks only during the warm months of the year. Otherwise hens and chicks must be confined where the warmth of a brooder light can be provided.

Diseases

Chilling in Baby Chicks: In this condition the chicks huddle together and cheep and chirp unhappily. Place a thermometer on the brooder floor near the brooder light. The temperature should be 95°F (35°C) for newly hatched chicks. In a commercial brooder the temperature is lowered five F degrees (2.8 C degrees) each week. As they get older and require less heat, chicks will move away from the warmest area of the bulb.

Fowl Pox: Chickens with fowl pox have wartlike scabs on their face, wattles (the reddish appendages that hang down under the beak), and comb. This is a virus infection spread from other poultry by mosquitoes.

Laying hens will stop laying, but chickens seldom die from this disease. Once the lesions heal, the chickens will begin laying again.

No treatment is required.

Enteritis: The primary symptom of enteritis is diarrhea. Instead of well-formed droppings, the chickens void foamy yellow or greenish material. In addition, the chickens themselves are droopy and depressed.

While this can be caused by an internal parasite, in pet chickens it is much more likely to be a bacterial infection.

If your chickens are confined to a coop or yard, both should be thoroughly cleaned. Perches should be scrubbed and waterers disinfected. All droppings should be removed.

This condition is usually effectively treated by giving antibiotics or sulfonamide drugs. I prefer tetracycline or chloramphenicol. The amount of medication given depends on the weight of the bird. We give fifty mg per pound (100 mg per kg) of body weight each day in divided doses. The chickens must be weighed and the proper dosage calculated.

If baby chicks are involved, the daily medication is mixed in a small amount of starter mash. Use the amount of mash the chicks will eat up during the daytime hours.

Older pet chickens are given this medication in capsules. Weigh the chicken to be treated. Calculate the dosage to be given twice daily, twenty-five mg per pound (55 mg per kg). Capsules come in 100 mg and 250 mg sizes. Choose the appropriate capsule. If necessary, open a capsule and discard a portion of the medication to have the proper amount.

Make the capsule slippery by coating it with butter or margarine, so the bird can more easily swallow it. Have someone assist you. He or she steadies the chicken by holding one hand on each side of its body, confining the wings. With one hand you open the beak and with the other you place the capsule in the back part of the mouth and poke it down the throat with your finger. The chicken will swallow. Treatment should be done twice daily. Two days after the droppings return to normal, stop treatment.

While giving capsules twice daily would be impractical for a poultry farmer, it is the best way for you to treat your few birds. This way you know that each bird is receiving the proper amount of medication at the proper time. After you have weighed your chickens, your veterinarian will supply the proper size capsules and specific medication for your situation.

Respiratory Infections: In this condition there is a discharge around the nostrils and frequently from the eyes. The chicken is droopy and depressed. The chicken sneezes, coughs, and in severe cases, gasps for air.

This is frequently a bacterial infection, also. Use the same antibiotics as in the treatment of enteritis. If the chicks are under eight or ten weeks of age, be sure a brooder light is provided to prevent them from becoming chilled. The light should be available for a week after treatment has been stopped.

Mites, Fleas, and Lice: These are external parasites that suck blood from your chickens. They make the birds uncomfortable and lower their resistance to other diseases.

Lice and fleas spend all their time on the chicken. Lice are seen as small grayish bugs crawling among the feathers close to the skin. They are most easily seen in the short feathers around the vent. Fleas are darker in color. They usually attach themselves to the skin around the eyes and under the wattles.

Mites are tiny, spiderlike creatures that live in cracks and crevices in the coop. They crawl out at night and suck blood from the chickens. You will frequently see these bugs crawling about on eggs in the nest. They cause intense itching and rough scaly legs on the chicken.

If you see or suspect any of these parasites, dust your chicken thoroughly with a 1.5 to 5 percent rotenone powder. In addition, the nests, perches, and coop should also be dusted well with this powder. Repeat this treatment once a week for three weeks. If rotenone is not available, usually any flea powder that is safe for cats can be used on chickens.

Internal Parasites: Internal parasites are seldom a problem in pet chickens. If you suspect your chickens may have worms or other internal parasites, gather a plastic vial full of droppings and have a microscopic parasite examination performed at your local veterinary hospital. If internal parasites are found, the proper medication will be prescribed.

Miscellaneous: There are other specific diseases, such as leucosis and coccidiosis, that are much more a problem to the poultry farmer who has hundreds of birds closely confined. A large group of birds is more susceptible to the spread of many diseases.

Chickens are surprisingly healthy. If, however, one of your chickens is not acting normally, contact your veterinarian. If he is not able to help you, he will refer you to someone who can.

For many years chickens have been regarded as dumb utilitarian creatures. But this attitude is changing. Researchers have found that chickens can be taught to perform simple tasks and problem solving to obtain food. This research now concludes what our family has known all along: that chickens aren't dumb after all.

No Reference and Suggested Reading list has been included at the end of this chapter because all the information given here is based on personal observation and knowledge gathered from many sources over the years.

8 / Ducks

Who would want a duck for a pet? My son Bill, for one. He has always liked ducks, and while he was growing up we always had one or more pet ducks. Why would you want a pet duck? For Bill, it's enough to say, "they are neat." For you, it can be that you admire a specific breed of duck, or that you want a pet that can live out of doors with little care and that welcomes your attention and company.

Ducks are gentle creatures. They must be protected from stray dogs and nighttime wild predators. Naturally, they enjoy water. And they are fairly safe in it at night, floating or roosting on a log out in the water.

It is not necessary to provide them with swimming water. Ducks are content to wander around a grassy yard in search of bugs. They will bask in the sun and play in whatever water you provide. A pail of water is used for drinking and partial bathing. A plastic dishpan of water makes for a delightful bath. A duck will climb into the pan, shake water onto its feathers, duck its head under the water, and flap its wings, scattering water everywhere. Afterward it will spend an hour preening—nibbling and straightening each feather with its bill. When the job is complete it will waddle about the yard again foraging for tender greens and available bugs.

While there are many types of waterfowl that make good pets, domestic ducks are the best. Wild ducks may not be kept unless you have state and federal permits to do so. When we raise wild ducks we do so with the understanding that they will be given their freedom when they are able to care for themselves. We do not raise them as pets.

Swans and geese can be terrors. They are aggressive and seem to enjoy bullying any creature that will run from them, including young children. They are also capable of giving painful nips with their beaks, a smack with their heavy wings, and scratches with their sharp toenails. They just aren't meant to be pets for young people.

There are eight or nine breeds of domestic ducks, but the two most popular domestic ducks are the white Pekin and the Muscovy. A third breed, the domestic mallard, also makes a good pet. It is similar to the wild mallard, but not as common.

The white Pekin duck originally came from China in about 1873. It is a fairly large duck, about eight to nine pounds (4 kg), with white plumage, and a yellow-orange bill, legs, and feet. It does not fly. It is raised by commercial breeders primarily as a meat bird.

The Muscovy duck comes from Brazil. Slightly smaller than the Pekin, Muscovy is black and white with a variety of plumage patterns. The distinctive characteristic is red lumps of tissue that literally covers the head, the area around the eyes, and portions of the neck. The Muscovys are strong flyers. They are attached to their home, but frequently will fly away to feed, returning later in the day. If they are treated with kindness they always return.

Muscovy ducks also are raised primarily as meat ducks. The females lay eggs in the springtime, their nesting time. If the

Female Muscovy duck (male pictured at beginning of chapter).

eggs aren't taken, the female will make a nest, lay a clutch of eggs, incubate, and hatch a bunch of ducklings each spring.

Muscovys are tame, gentle ducks. They cannot quack or make any noise except for a quiet hissing sound of greeting.

Both Pekins and Muscovys make fine pets. Get your duck when it is just a day or two old if you wish it to be quite tame. If you wish a very dependent pet, get just one duckling. It will need your companionship and want a lot of attention.

Two or three can keep each other company. While they are more independent, they will still be glad to see you.

Ducklings at this age will imprint, or become attached, to you. You will be their mother. They look to you for their care and food. They will follow you wherever you go, and, unless you betray their trust, will always regard you as their leader and friend.

Housing

Housing should be all set up when you bring your ducklings home. They have the same basic requirements of warmth, food, water, and protection from predators and weather as do chickens. Prepare a brooder cage with a 60-watt bulb for warmth and jar lids for food and water. A brooder two feet wide, two feet long, and one foot high (60 × 60 × 30 cm) is fine for three to six ducklings. While a large cardboard box can be used, a wooden cage is better. The bottom and at least two of the sides should be of solid material such as exterior plywood. The other two sides can be of half-inch-mesh hardware-cloth. The solid sides protect the ducklings from drafts. The hardware-cloth sides provide ventilation and allow the babies to see out. Place a top on the brooder to protect the ducklings from cats or other predators.

Purchase a porcelain ceiling light fixture from any hardware store to hold the bulb that provides warmth. Cover exposed wires with electrician's tape. Place the fixture in a protected corner, sheltered from drafts, and put a thermometer near it.

The brooder cage, with pool, jar waterer, growing mash, and light bulb.

Porcelain ceiling fixture placed on the floor of the cage provides all the warmth the babies need.

The temperature on the floor near the 60-watt bulb should be 95°F (35°C). If it isn't that warm, use a larger light bulb. The ducklings will move in close to the light for warmth when they need it. They will use this extra warmth until they are four to six weeks old.

Cover the bottom of the entire cage with papers and change them when they become messy.

We offer our ducklings a chance to go swimming several times a day. An eight-by-eleven-inch aluminum cake pan, two inches deep (20 × 28 × 5 cm), makes a good pond. Fill it with fresh clean water each time, and remove the pan at the end of the swimming session. Until they are a week old, the swimming sessions should not be over ten to fifteen minutes long.

If you leave the swimming pool in the brooder too long, it is harmful. The babies stay in the water continuously, chill, and some die. It is important that they learn to enjoy the water at an early age. But they should not be allowed in the water for more than fifteen minutes at a time until they are old enough to be less dependent on their light for warmth.

Do not place the swimming pool too close to their brooder light. The ducklings splash water while bathing, and it only takes a few drops of water to make the light bulb burst.

As the ducklings get older, and when the weather is warm, their swimming time can be extended. Their brooder cage should be moved out on the grass during the warm part of the day. Tip the brooder cage on its side so the grass coming through the hardware-cloth side becomes the bottom of their outdoor pen. The ducklings will feed on the tender shoots of grass and will attack and eat any bugs they see. The brooder light should be kept in the cage and plugged in, so the ducklings stay warm.

Allow them their freedom outside the brooder when they are outdoors at three weeks of age and older. Open the top (which is now acting as a side) to let them out. The brooder represents security and food, and the ducklings will stay close to it. At this

Baby ducks in their swimming pool—an aluminum cake pan.

age they don't need their light during the day, but still require it on chilly, damp nights.

When it is time for the ducklings to go in, herd them into the brooder and tip it up to its normal position. Move the brooder cage indoors, place clean papers in the bottom, plug in their light, and give them food and water.

When they are eight weeks old give them the freedom of the yard. If the weather is reasonably warm, they will no longer need their light. At this age they need a semipermanent shelter and pen for nighttime security and as a protection against severe weather.

I favor a pen that can be moved periodically. It need only be about six feet (2 meters) on each side, and three feet (1 meter) tall. This is long enough for three or four ducks. Most of the sides should be of welded wire mesh fastened to a wooden framework. Welded wire mesh is strong enough to keep out predators. The pen should have a duck-sized door two feet (60 cm) wide that can be latched to protect your duckings. One end of the pen should have wooden walls and a roof to form a shed that will give protection from rain and cold. No perch is necessary, for ducks rest on the ground.

The pen should also have a welded wire top to protect the ducklings from predators. With no bottom on the pen, it can be picked up and moved to fresh ground or grass every week or so.

Place feeders and a waterer in the pen, so your ducks get used to entering it. At night they may be herded into the pen and the door latched until morning for their own protection.

In winter, in snowy areas, cover the roof and a portion of the sides with plastic to keep the snow out of the pen. Situate the pen so the solid wall provides the ducks with maximum protection from the prevailing cold winds. They have warm plumage and will survive very well as long as they have some protection, adequate food, and unfrozen water for drinking.

In our area—Florida—the winter housing is not a problem. Since we also live on a lake the ducks have no pen as such, but stay on the lake at night. We have raccoon, foxes, and other creatures about, but the ducks manage very well without additional protection.

Our ducks spend a great deal of time on the water, but each morning and each afternoon when our boys come home from school, the ducks can be counted on to come to the house for food and attention.

Feeding

Baby ducklings should be offered mash in a jar lid placed close to their light. However, instead of chicken starter mash, which we use for baby chicks, we feed ducklings the chicken growing mash. Some chicken starter mash has medication in it that is not required for ducks. The growing mash works well and contains all the nutrients the duckling needs.

In addition to the mash in the jar lid we place a few bits about on their paper, and also sprinkle a few pieces in the jar lid containing water. The baby ducklings learn to eat quickly by chasing the bits of food floating on the water. Their instinct is to feed on materials floating in the water, and they can't resist the piece of mash that floats in their water dish. They also quickly learn to feed on the bits that sink to the bottom of the shallow water container.

However, as soon as they learn that the mash is food and they are eating well, remove the jar lids as waterers. Although they only have about a third of an inch (1 cm) of water in them, they are a temptation the ducklings can't resist. They climb into them, bathe in them, try to swim in them, and at times eliminate in them. Because the ducklings splash water about, and because the water quickly becomes dirty, the lids should be replaced as soon as possible with an inverted mason jar waterer that can be purchased at the feed store. The ducklings can't get in the water supplied in the inverted quart mason jar, which provides a more dependable source of clean water.

Since we allow our ducklings a chance to eat green grass and other tidbits they find when out of doors, the only food we offer is the growing mash.

If you must keep your ducklings confined for some reason, offer them a little bit of lettuce or celery tops each day. Green food is important. Be sure the greens have been rinsed thoroughly before they are given to the ducklings. One leaf of lettuce for each duckling once a day is plenty. This green vegetable supplement should be supplied every day unless the ducks are loose where they can find their own "growing greens."

When your ducks are mature, you can keep the growing mash available in their pen at all times in a troughlike feeder. Place the feeder in the sheltered shed portion where it will be protected from the rain.

If your ducks have access to water and don't spend much time at the pen, it is easier to offer them a small amount of mash several times a day. Offer about a quarter of a cup to each duck in the morning and again in the afternoon. A flat board placed on the ground works fine as a feeding table. It doesn't take long for your ducks to settle into this routine of feeding. They soon know when to expect you and will be waiting at their table for you to appear, so be consistent.

Since free roaming adult ducks find a large portion of their own food, we usually feed mixed bird grain instead of mash when they are grown. We always have bird grain on hand, and it keeps better than the mash in our damp climate.

The ducks know that my wife, Barbara, will be outside first thing in the morning, so they are there to greet her. She feeds them in the morning, and the boys or I feed them in the late afternoon.

We enjoy seeing ducks floating serenely on the lake and enjoy having them waddle up the lawn to the house to come and pay a visit.

Breeding

A male duck is called a drake, a female is a hen. Drake mallards have the brightly colored male plumage that distinguishes them from the plainer brown females. Muscovy drakes are considerably larger than the hens and have many more of the red bumps

Quiet, gentle birds, Muscovy ducks enjoy company, attention, and food.

on their heads and necks. The white Pekin drakes look very similar to the hens, but the males have small forward curling tail feathers at the base of the tail, while the hens have a smooth top line all the way to the tip of the tail.

If you are raising ducklings, you must have both a drake and a hen to have fertile eggs. In the spring the hen will make a nest and lay her eggs. If your ducks use a pen, make a nest box for each hen in the protected and sheltered portion. The nest need only be a wooden box eighteen inches (45 cm) on each side, with an open end, or entrance, facing the center of the pen. Place hay, straw, or grass clippings in the nest box for nest material. The nest box will offer protection from the weather and a feeling of security for the hen.

If you intend to hatch just a few ducklings, let the mother duck do it for you. A hen will not start to incubate her eggs in earnest until she has a full clutch of eight to twelve eggs. For if she were to start incubating when the first egg was laid, one duckling would hatch each day instead of the whole clutch hatching at once. It would be impossible for a hen to manage ducklings of all ages that were running about while she still tried to incubate the remaining eggs. By waiting till the clutch is complete to begin incubating, she hatches all the ducklings the same day. She will, however, sit on the nest for a short period each day as she lays an additional egg. This short period keeps the eggs warm enough to remain viable, but does not really start development of the embryo.

For most ducks it takes twenty-eight days from the start of incubation till they have their coming-out party. However, Muscovy eggs hatch in thirty-three to thirty-five days, so figure on five or six extra days for them. You can mark each egg with the date it is placed in the incubator, or you may add twenty-eight days to the date—or thirty-three for a Muscovy—and write the date the egg is to be hatched.

If you use an incubator to hatch your fertile duck eggs, follow the manufacturer's directions. Duck eggs are usually incubated at about 100°F (37.8 C°). The humidity in the incubator should be high. A damp cloth or a shallow tray of water must be kept in the incubator at all times.

The eggs must be turned at least twice daily. Four or five times per day during the first three weeks is even better. The bottom of the egg where it is resting on the floor of the incubator is rotated until it becomes the topmost part of the egg. If possible, position the egg so the small end is the lowest portion of the egg.

We know that the hen communicates with the babies while they are still in the egg. They answer her quiet vocalizing with tiny peeps that can be heard through the shell. It is believed by many that the hen uses these vocal signals to induce the babies to begin breaking out of the shell. It also encourages slow hatchers.

If you use an incubator to hatch your baby ducklings, lift each egg as hatching time approaches. Make a vocal "peep" at the eggs. If you hold the egg near your ear when you do this you will frequently hear an answering peep from the egg. This is another way of imprinting the baby ducklings on you. When they hatch, they will know your voice. As far as they are concerned, you are their mother. They will follow you and come to your voice.

Being a mother duck is a responsibility. You have to keep your children warm, be certain they have food and water, teach them to eat and swim, and protect them till they are mature enough to protect themselves.

Diseases

There are few specific diseases that domestic pet ducks incur. They are remarkably healthy.

Mites or Lice: Occasionally if pet ducks contact other birds or wild ducks, they may acquire mites or lice.

If you see any tiny insects crawling about on your duck's feathers, or on the skin on the inside of the wings, these could be mites.

Thoroughly dust 1.5 to 5 percent rotenone powder into the feathers and down once a week.

Diarrhea: A duck's droppings are normally quite loose and runny. If however, they appear foamy or yellow in color or contain blood this can be serious in young birds.

Usually the only treatment is to make things in the brooder as clean as possible. Change the papers in the brooder at least three or four times daily instead of once. Clean the waterer thoroughly each day. Try to be certain no food is contaminated with bowel material.

If the bowel movements aren't normal in twenty-four to thirty-six hours consult your veterinarian.

Botulism: This fatal toxic condition is caused by a bacterial organism. Stagnant warm water in shallow ponds favors the growth of the botulism organism.

Ducks that drink water containing this toxin stagger and appear to be uncoordinated or drunk. They progress quickly to the point where they can't walk or even lift their heads off the ground. The common name for this disease at this stage is limber neck. Most affected ducks die. If you have more than one duck, pen all the other ducks away from the contaminated water.

Affected ducks may be given epsom salts (magnesium sulfate) by stomach tube if you feel sure of yourself. One teaspoonful (5 grams) of epsom salt in an ounce (30 ml) of water should flush the contents from the intestinal tract, eliminating some of the toxin.

This condition is not seen frequently.

If your ducks are given reasonable care, clean surroundings, and food to supplement what they themselves find, you can expect them to live to a ripe old age of ten to twelve years. The pet duck will repay your care with persistent devotion and unswerving friendship.

No Reference and Suggested Reading list has been included at the end of this chapter because all the information given here is based on personal observation and knowledge gathered from many different sources over the years.

9 / Frogs, Toads, and Salamanders

A pet frog, toad, or salamander is different from most pets. While all are amphibians, and many individuals have their own temperaments and personalities, this group is not regarded as being either affectionate or particularly intelligent. Toads are considered more intelligent than frogs or salamanders. Many of them learn to come regularly when called, eat food offered, and then move forward in position to have their backs gently rubbed. The most that can be said for frogs and salamanders is that some of them learn to accept tidbits of food from their owners' hands. The true value in keeping these creatures is in learning more about their normal habits and behavior.

With their long prehensile tongues, frogs and toads feed on insects and other moving objects. Both have strong rear legs for jumping, lay their eggs in water, and have other points in common. However, the differences between them are quite obvious. Frogs have smooth moist skin, and they are slender and live near or in water. Toads have a pebbly, dry, warty skin, they are chunky in shape, and they return to the water only at mating time. Salamanders are lizardlike, with a smooth, moist skin.

In spite of these differences, the care and feeding of frogs and toads is essentially the same. Salamanders have requirements for care very similar to those of frogs.

The word *amphibian* is derived from the Greek *amphi* and *bios*, meaning "double life." It refers to creatures that start life in water and later adapt to life on land. Frogs, toads, and salamanders lay their eggs in water. The young emerge from the egg and live in water. The young of frogs and toads are known as tadpoles or polliwogs. With growth and other changes, called *metamorphosis*, they move to land as miniature frogs and toads.

Amphibians that adapt best to observation are the tamest individuals, and the tamest frogs and toads are those that are captured as tadpoles. They learn to accept human association as part of their normal existence. Tadpoles can be captured in the warm shallow water of ponds, in semipermanent puddles, and along lake edges in late spring and early summer.

Within the order Salientia, or "leaping ones," there are 18 families, 250 genera, and 2,500 species. In the United States there are about one hundred species of frogs and toads and two hundred species of salamanders, so you must use all the information you can find to identify your creature properly.

It is difficult to look at a tadpole captured from the water and know what type of frog or toad you will have. While it is true that the tadpole of a bullfrog will be large and that most toad tadpoles are black, it takes an expert to identify most of them correctly. You must wait until the tadpole grows into its final form and acquires the colors it will wear as an adult.

The color patterns and physical appearance are the primary method of identifying the particular species.

The color of a frog's or toad's skin is determined by chromatophores, which are pigmented cells of the skin. These cells have the ability to concentrate or disperse the pigment granules within the cells. By changing the grouping and concentration of pigment granules, many amphibians change shades of color. Toads may be light or dark, or a tree frog may appear tan or green.

Distinctive physical characteristics, such as the suckerlike pads on the toes of tree frogs, are important. The eyes, which usually have rich yellow-colored irises in most toads and frogs, are also used in identification. Both the color of the iris and the shape of the pupil must be noted. The spadefoot toad, for example, has a vertical pupil rather than the round pupil of other toads, and the iris of the spadefoot is a deep gold color rather than yellow.

The location and type of *habitat* where your specimen was found is also vital information.

Some frogs, such as the mink frogs, have a strong pungent odor from glands in the skin. Others smell like garlic or vanilla. This odor is a protective mechanism for the frog, but for you, it is the kind of fact that will help you to be certain of your identification.

Experts rely on the sounds a frog or toad makes to help in identification. Each species has its own particular call. The high-pitched cheeping of the spring peeper is far different from the deep "jug-of-rum" grunting of the bullfrog.

Salamanders vary a great deal in size, from two inches (5 cm) up to thirty-nine (1 meter) in length. However, the majority are less than six inches (15 cm) long. Some look more like eels and spend their entire life in the water, while others look like lizards and return to the water only to breed. Some salamanders breathe through gills, others through lungs, while some get the oxygen they need through their skin. Color, size, shape, and habitat are all important points in identification.

All of the information you acquire about your amphibian will help firm up your tentative identification.

As you come to know more about these creatures, you cannot help but revise the popular notions about frogs and toads. Even today the word "toad" may mean something ugly or evil to some people. If offered minimum protection, a toad will stake out a territory around your home or garden and eat the insects and slugs that attack your plants. Instead of believing that touching a toad causes warts, you will learn that toads have a potent secretion from specific glands in the skin that makes them taste bad to many predators. While it does protect them from predators, it does not cause disease in people.

Toads have been persecuted because they were considered evil, and frogs have been pursued as study models and as food. For centuries, because of ignorance, both creatures have suffered. And yet, they ask only to be left alone and in return aid us by removing great numbers of offensive insects.

Frogs do not live as long as toads. In her book, Hilda Simon talks of a toad that lived under the steps in an English garden for thirty-six years. It would come out when called to have its back scratched and then return to its protected spot during the daylight hours. But the life span of *Rana pipiens*, the leopard frog, is fifteen years. To observe and study even one individual in captivity can involve a number of years of care.

General information can be gathered by observing a frog in the wild. Yet captivity is essential to the study of a specific individual over a period of time.

Captivity, while it is essential to certain studies, also involves responsibility for proper care. The creature must be fed properly, kept clean, and offered room to exercise. Large frogs and toads are excellent jumpers. They need a great deal of space if they are to get sufficient exercise.

People who work with frogs and toads feel that they can tell by the way a toad or frog acts if it is happy and content. An "unhappy" prisoner should be freed as soon as possible. If it droops in an isolated corner, doesn't eat, appears dull in color, and shows no sparkle in the eye, take it back where you found it and release it while it can still adapt to the free wild life.

Handling

To pick up a large frog or toad, gently place your hand around its body just behind the forelegs. Don't squeeze the creature's body, but hold it firmly enough for it not to wiggle free. Do not hold it by its back legs. As it lunges to escape, it can seriously injure the lower back or hip joints.

Smaller frogs can be confined and carried by making a cup-like cavity of your two hands. Until your frog or toad gets used to you and to being carried in this fashion, do not allow any openings in the confining fingers through which it can jump. For it will try to escape when first handled. As it becomes more accustomed to you, it becomes more tolerant of handling.

It is best not to handle a new captive amphibian any more than is absolutely necessary the first couple of days. Give it a chance to adapt to its new home, and then spend time getting acquainted.

If you must transport a frog or toad some distance, a cloth sack, or even a sock, moistened and filled with soft damp moss or leaves will serve as a carrying container.

A frightened toad will inflate its body with air. It will tuck its head down on its chin and pull its legs in close to its body, making it appear to be almost round in shape. This makes it appear larger and more difficult to pick up. Cup both hands around it, and hold it gently until it relaxes and deflates.

Toads seem to accept handling more readily than frogs. Some of the tree frogs become accustomed to people and handling, but most frogs always try to escape.

To handle your salamander, moisten your hand first, for most salamanders have a soft tender skin. Grasp it firmly but gently around the body. If you grasp one by the tail, the tail usually will come off in your hand. While the salamander can grow a new tail, it should not be necessary for it to do so. To transport a salamander any distance, place it in a plastic bag containing water and moistened leaves.

Housing

Try to provide an environment similar to that which your amphibian lived in when it was free. Note the types of plants, grass, and shrubs in the area where you captured it. Duplicate its living accommodations by bringing home leaves, soil, bark, rocks, plants, and even water.

Probably the best container for pet amphibians is the ordinary rectangular aquarium. The larger the aquarium, the better the habitat you can make. A tank one foot (30 cm) wide and high and two feet (60 cm) long is the minimum size suitable for all but the largest specimens. Large toads and frogs need space to jump and exercise in, and any aquarium that would be adequate for their needs would be much too large for the average home.

There are three main habitats for these amphibians: an aquatic aquarium for tadpoles or polliwogs; a semiaquatic terrarium for salamanders and frogs that live in water; and a woodland terrarium for woodland frogs and toads.

The aquarium for tadpoles is a true aquarium. Since they live entirely in the water, no land area is required. To prepare your aquarium for the tadpoles, place an inch of pebbles or small rocks in the bottom of the aquarium. Then add sand at one end to make a sloping shore that tapers up toward one end of the tank. The water need be only one to two inches (2.5–5 cm) deep. However, the sloping shore constructed at one end is most important. The tadpoles rest in the shallow water, and this is where they will also be fed.

It is safest for your tadpoles if the water used to fill the aquarium is from the spot where you captured them. If this is not practical, tap water may be used. It must be properly dechlorinated before you use it. The chlorine added to treated municipal water must be allowed to evaporate from the water. Placing the water in open containers for at least two days will make it safe.

Place a few rocks or logs from the area where you captured your tadpoles on the sloping shore. The rocks or logs provide hiding and resting places for the tadpoles. Last, the water plants and algae you collected are placed in the water. When the water settles and loses some of its turbidity, add your tadpoles. Several pond snails may be added to keep your tank clean.

The temperature of the water in the tank should be 72° to

75°F (22°–24°C) for northern tadpoles, and 77° to 80°F (25°–27°C) for southern tadpoles. The water should be changed every three days to eliminate waste products and the remains of spoiled, uneaten food. An inexpensive siphon can be used to remove the old water.

As soon as the tadpoles begin to show definite legs, increase the land area of your aquarium. The metamorphosing tadpoles will crawl out on solid objects such as rocks or logs partially submerged in the shallow water.

When you see that the tadpoles are changing into miniature frogs or toads, it is time to change the aquarium to a semi-aquatic habitat. This means that about half of your aquarium will be land and half will be water.

With aquarium cement, cement a piece of plate glass in the bottom of the aquarium to partition and divide the aquarium into equal watertight halves.

Make the height of your glass partition one-third the height of your aquarium. Obtain the proper size piece of glass at the hardware store. Half of the aquarium will be water habitat as before, and the other half will be made into a woodland habitat.

Set up the land area by placing an inch (2.5 cm) layer of pebbles or gravel in the bottom first, then an inch (2.5 cm) layer of rock or broken flowerpots, and a similar layer of charcoal. Next add two to three inches (5–8 cm) of sandy loam, and last one to two inches (2.5–5 cm) of topsoil. Scatter a few leaves or bits of bark on the soil. Plant several woodland plants, ferns, and mosses in the topsoil. Try to make the woodland portion of your terrarium as natural-looking as possible.

If the semiaquatic terrarium is for frogs, the water portion must be deep enough for the adult frog living in the terrarium to float in the water with its legs extended and hanging downward without touching the bottom. The water should be changed about every three days. Amphibians absorb substances through their skin. If toxic waste products are allowed to build up in the water, they will poison your frog.

A simple siphon can be used to remove the water into one or more gallon jugs. Waste water should be flushed down the toilet or used to fertilize plants out of doors. Do not pour it down the sink your family uses. Use fresh dechlorinated water to refill the aquarium.

Since frogs and toads can hop and jump, the semiaquatic terrarium must have a cover. A piece of window screen does fine. If you plan to have your terrarium on a porch or out of doors, hardware-cloth for the top is better. This wider mesh allows insects to enter the terrarium and furnishes natural food to the occupants.

Prepare a semiaquatic terrarium for your salamander as for frogs. Even the woodland or land variety salamanders frequently enter the water. Place logs, rocks, and leaves in your terrarium as a hiding place for your salamander. Just as for frogs, it is important that the water portion of your terrarium be cleaned regularly and the replacement water be dechlorinated. The mosses, ferns, and plants in all terrariums should be watered daily with a mist-spray waterer, using dechlorinated water. Since salamanders are good climbers, it is essential to have a well-fitting top for your terrarium. Either window screens or plate glass may be used. The ideal terrarium temperature for salamanders should be from 60° to 70°F (16°–21°C).

To make a woodland terrarium for toads or woodland frogs, prepare the entire aquarium exactly as described in the preparation of the land portion of the semiaquatic terrarium. Although there is no water portion, you must provide water in your woodland terrarium. Since amphibians satisfy their water needs by absorbing water through their skin, place a bowl that will be deep enough for your captive to immerse its entire body in a hole of the proper size at one end of the terrarium. The edge of the bowl should be even with the ground level.

All terrariums should be kept moist and not be allowed to dry out. Frogs and toads may live for weeks without food, but they will die in a few days without water. Water your terrarium daily with a mist waterer using dechlorinated water. Keep the soil moist. But never add so much water that it completely covers and fills the pebble layer in the bottom of the terrarium.

Frog in woodland terrarium is as comfortable as in the wild, but safer from predators.

You can monitor the water level through the glass side of your terrarium.

You must also place a small feeding dish in the terrarium. A shallow saucer works well. Place worms and crawling insects, which are used as food, on this dish. If they are placed directly on the soil, some will immediately dig in and hide before your friend can find them.

The terrarium should be kept at a temperature of 70° to 80°F (21°–27°C) for frogs and toads. Keep a thermometer in your terrarium with the bulb at about ground level at all times. Then you will know that the temperature is correct. If you find the temperature frequently goes below 65°F (18°C), add a light bulb for heat.

In one corner suspend a 60-watt bulb for warmth. When it

is cool the creatures will move close and bask in the warmth of the light. If your terrarium is outdoors or on a porch, the light will serve an additional purpose. It will attract many night-flying insects. Your frog or toad will feast each night on these insects that come through the openings in the hardware-cloth top.

During the winter, northern toads and frogs hibernate. If you live in the north, it is best to place your terrarium in a cool spot outdoors in the late fall. Toads will burrow into the ground to hibernate, while frogs will burrow into the mud or soil in the aquatic area of your terrarium. At 40°F (4°C) and below, toads and frogs stop breathing and absorb what little oxygen they need through the skin. The terrarium should be protected from hard freezes but allowed to stay in the cool spot until spring.

If your occupants are southern frogs or toads, they should be kept in a warm spot year round. As long as your temperature is in the 70s F (20s C) they will be active. Normally even in the south the temperature falls below 40°F (4°C) at times during the winter. When it does, native southern frogs hibernate, too. But as soon as the temperature comes back up they come out and are active again.

The terrarium or aquarium should not be placed in direct sunlight for any length of time. A little sun is good. It warms the soil and helps the plants grow. But a terrarium will get too hot if left in the sun for several hours. In these high temperatures, the inhabitants of a microenvironment will frequently die.

You may keep more than one creature in your terrarium at one time. But don't overcrowd it. If frogs and toads are in the same terrarium, they should be of about the same size, for large frogs and toads have a habit of eating their smaller relatives.

Practically all toads and frogs are solitary creatures except during the mating season. Normally each stakes out a territory and will fight or drive a rival away. Two or three toads in a small aquarium will make it a constant battleground.

If more than one creature is to be placed in the terrarium, it would be best to use different species. A toad and a tortoise would be compatible. A toad and a similar-sized frog would be fine in a semiaquatic aquarium. A couple of tree frogs, or hyla, are small enough to have enough room for separate territories. Under no circumstances should a snake be placed in a terrarium with any toads or frogs, for the snake will quickly eat them.

A pickerel frog should not be kept in a semiaquatic aquarium with any other frogs. Pickerel frogs have a secretion from their skin that is toxic to other frogs. This secretion can be irritating to the eyes and skin of some people. It is a good idea to wash your hands thoroughly after handling any frogs, toads, or salamanders.

Two last points. Cleanliness is most important if you are to have healthy creatures in your terrarium. Change the water on a regular schedule, and clean the rest of the terrarium as often as needed. Second, insecticides cannot be used around your terrarium. They will not only kill the creatures that toads and frogs feed on, but will kill the amphibians as well.

Keep a notebook of your terrarium; carefully keep a record of food habits, temperatures, behavior during different seasons of the year, and other details of your creature's daily life. Details that you notice and jot down might prove to be new and useful knowledge to the scientific world. You and your unusual pet may make a significant contribution to understanding amphibians better.

Feeding

Most toads, frogs, and salamanders are insect eaters. But a large bullfrog will eat a small bird, mouse, or fish if it can catch it and get it into its mouth. A toad will enjoy some snails, slugs, and earthworms. A salamander may be taught to eat bits of dog food, but in nature insects and worms make up the majority of its daily food.

Tadpoles thrive on any soft vegetable or animal protein. In the wild they feed primarily on algae, aquatic plant life, and any dead animal matter they can find. In your aquarium they can be fed bits of boiled lettuce, high-protein baby cereal, bits of egg yolk, rabbit food pellets, bits of dry dog food, and many other foods.

When the tadpoles change to miniature frogs and toads, they will no longer eat foods of this type. Only moving food attracts them. In the wild at this age, they search for insects such as mosquitoes and fruit flies. In your terrarium you can offer your young amphibians baby crickets, which can be obtained from a fishing bait supplier, earthworms which you dig up, or meal worms which are available at most pet stores.

If none of these live prey are available, try to offer food in a way that mimics flying insects. A small bit of Purina Cat Chow can be moistened until it is slightly soft. The bit can be impaled on a broom straw, weed stem, or a piece of thread. This bit of food is dangled in front of your toad or frog. If you are lucky, it will flip its tongue out and eat the proffered bit. If it eats one bite, each succeeding offering will be more readily accepted.

Adult amphibians need large numbers of insects as daily food. There are numerous fly traps available. If you are careful, these flies may be released in the terrarium without escaping all over the house.

It is also possible to raise flies. This is how: Place a piece of spoiled meat on a rack an inch (2.5 cm) above an aluminum cake pan that contains two inches (5 cm) of moist sand. Flies will lay eggs on the meat. The larva, or maggots, hatch from the eggs and feed on the spoiled meat. When they are mature, the larva drop off the meat onto the sand. They burrow into the sand and pupate. You must sift the sand each day and harvest these pupae. Collect them in a jar and place the jar in the refrigerator. When you need flies for food for your amphibian, place several of the pupae on the feeding dish in your terrarium. At room temperature the flies will emerge from the cocoonlike pupae in two or three days.

The insect sources of food are unlimited. The number and type you collect depends on where you live and your own ingenuity. Grasshoppers and moths may be gathered in grassy fields by using a butterfly net. As you walk through the field, pass the net back and forth ahead of you at grass-top level scooping up the insects you scare up.

Crickets and earthworms may be purchased from fish bait dealers. Some commercial earthworms may not be palatable to your frogs and toads. It is better to dig up your own earthworms, or collect them in the lawn after a rain, or search for them under piles of accumulated moist leaves. The earthworms you collect may be kept in a wooden box until needed.

A box one foot (30 cm) square is a good size. Fill the box three-quarters full of soil, rotted leaf humus, and a covering of leaves. Keep the soil moist, but not wet. The earthworms keep indefinitely at 65°F (18°C). Two tablespoonfuls of corn meal or rolled oats can be added and worked into the soil once a week to feed the worms. If you have quite a few that you feed well, you may soon find that you are growing many baby earthworms in the holding box.

Meal worms can be purchased from most pet stores. They can be dangled in front of your frog or toad on a straw or from a forceps. If the worms are healthy and are moving about, place them in the feeding dish where the movement will attract your frog or toad.

Crickets are turned loose in the terrarium. By offering different types of insects, you can vary the diet.

Frogs or toads that will not eat may be force-fed. Use a rubber-tipped forceps to poke crickets or earthworms down the throat of your frog or toad. The amount to feed depends on the size of the animal. Usually a couple of crickets or earthworms are enough for a medium-sized toad or frog.

Restraining a toad and forcing food into it will not make a good trusting relationship or a happy critter. It is preferable to set such a frog or toad free.

I find it is easiest to feed a toad or frog by placing the terrarium out of doors where they can catch their own food. The hardware-cloth top keeps the frog or toad in, but allows insects to enter. A light in the terrarium will attract flying insects and give additional warmth on cool nights.

In nature salamanders eat insects, earthworms, leeches, small crustaceans, frog and fish eggs, and other animals small enough for it to swallow. In your terrarium most salamanders will do well if fed small earthworms twice weekly. If earthworms are not available, tubifex worms (a small aquatic worm available at many pet shops), meal worms, any small insects you can catch, along with bits of canned dog food or liver, can be used.

Like frogs and toads, salamanders accept wiggling moving food best. But most can be taught to eat other things.

Many salamanders adapt well to life in a terrarium. They learn to anticipate feeding time and will run to the feeding dish and be waiting for you. If you can teach them to eat canned dog food or moistened Cat Chow, your feeding chores will be much easier and you will have won a major battle in helping these interesting creatures keep well and healthy.

If your salamander doesn't adapt, as evidenced by not eating in two or three days, take it back and release it exactly where you found it.

Breeding

Egg laying by toads and frogs occurs in late spring and early summer. Normally, after a warm spring rain, male frogs and toads congregate in the shallow waters of the ponds at dusk and begin to sing. Their singing attracts the females, who follow the sound to where the males wait.

When the female approaches, the male, usually smaller, clasps her from behind. In tandem they move into the water. The female lays eggs which are fertilized by the male as they are laid. Once the eggs are laid, the pair usually separates. A batch of bullfrog eggs will number from 10,000 to 25,000.

The eggs hatch quickly in warm water but may take weeks to hatch if the water is cold. The time of metamorphosis from egg to tadpole to frog may be as short as ten to twelve days. Or, in the bullfrog, it may take as long as a year, with another four years before the bullfrog is mature.

While a toad may lay 28,000 eggs in a year's time, the enemies of these creatures are many, and few toads grow to be adults.

Male toad, singing to attract a female.

Mating toads—male is smaller, at left.

If you wish to raise or breed frogs or toads, you may confine a male and a female in your semiaquatic terrarium in the fall. They will have a chance to adapt to the terrarium before the breeding season arrives in spring.

It may be difficult to tell the difference between males and females. In general, males are smaller. In many species of frogs the tympanic membrane that covers the ear canal just behind the eye is larger than the eye in the males. In females, the tympanum is smaller or the same size as the eye. Male tree frogs have a fold or vocal sac under their chin, for it is the male that does all the singing.

But the best way to be certain you have a pair would be to capture them at the time of mating. Concentration is so intense at that time, the breeding creatures will usually ignore a flashlight beam. If you move slowly and cautiously, you can get close enough to capture a pair. Place the pair in the water of your terrarium. They will lay eggs almost at once, unless they have already done so.

Raising bullfrogs and other frogs in outdoor ponds is a special project and beyond the scope of this book.

Once they have adapted, salamanders will usually breed, lay eggs, or raise young in your terrarium. Most egg laying is in the winter. You must watch for it and be careful not to siphon out the eggs when you change the water, for most salamanders lay their eggs in water. Some attach their eggs to twigs under the water, while the eggs of others float on the water's surface.

The larval form that hatches from the eggs looks like a miniature small salamander. It is usually an aquatic form, usually has gills, and lives entirely in the water. Some salamanders, such as the red eft, have an intermediate form that leaves the water to live on land, and then in its adult stage returns to the water. But many adult salamanders become terrestial or land creatures when they mature.

Remember to keep a notebook and jot down the points of behavior and life activities of these rather shy woodland and water creatures.

Watching the metamorphosis of egg to adult amphibian is one of the wonders of nature that you can observe in your own home.

Diseases

Shedding Skin: As they grow and mature, all amphibians shed their skin. While not a disease, this condition may alarm those who are not familiar with it.

Toads are easier to observe, since they spend their life on land. A young growing toad may shed as often as once a week. As adults they still shed, but only about three times a year.

The process starts with several large yawns. This apparently loosens the outer skin on the face. The toad will stretch and twist its body, hump its back and wiggle, until the loose skin looks as if it is a plastic raincoat over its body. Then with its forelegs it stuffs the loose skin around the face into its mouth. It continues pulling the thin sheet of skin off the body and stuffs it into its mouth until all the old skin has been swallowed. The new exposed skin looks shiny and clean, with the colors much more vivid and brighter.

Tumors: Five to ten percent of northern wild toads have kidney tumors called Locke tumors. This was the first tumor proven to be caused by a virus organism. It eventually causes death; there is no effective treatment.

Red Leg (Aeromonas infection): This disease is the major cause of death in laboratory frogs. It is caused by a bacterial organism, *Aeromonas hydrophila.* This organism is normally found in standing water. A healthy frog is usually not susceptible to this organism, but a captive distressed by new surroundings and inadequate food frequently becomes infected. A sick frog crawls instead of jumps and has red blotches on the skin which show up most clearly on the pale skin on the inside of the thighs. This red color gave the disease its name. Treatment with antibiotics does help if started early. Tetracycline is given by stomach tube twice daily for six days. The frog must be weighed, and the proper dose of 5 mg of tetracycline per ounce (30 grams) of frog is given in liquid twice daily. This antibiotic may be obtained from your veterinarian or on his prescription at the drugstore.

George Porter, another lover of frogs and toads, puts into words his philosophy on keeping frogs and toads:

"Frogs and toads are creatures of the wild. While many of them do well in captivity, it should be kept in mind that they do not really belong there. Keep a few of them if you must. Enjoy them and give them the best care possible. If you are not prepared or able to do so, leave them where they are. Wild animals are not toys."

I agree.

References and Suggested Reading

Conant, Isabelle H. *A Field Guide to Reptiles and Amphibians.* Boston: Houghton Mifflin, 1958.

Dolensek, Emil P., and Barbara Burn. *A Practical Guide to Impractical Pets.* New York: Viking Press, 1976.

Porter, George. *The World of the Frog and the Toad.* Philadelphia: J. B. Lippincott, 1967.

Simon, Hilda. *Frogs and Toads of the World.* Philadelphia: J. B. Lippincott, 1975.

Snedigar, Robert. *Our Small Native Animals: Their Habits and Care.* New York: Dover Publications, 1963.

Williams, Christine. *Practical Guide to Laboratory Animals.* St. Louis: C. V. Mosby Co., 1976.

10 / Turtles and Tortoises

A great many people use the word *turtle* to mean any animal whose four legs, head, and tail protrude from a shell that covers the back and abdomen. If you are to be a turtle fancier, you have to have the knowledge to be more specific than that.

All turtles, tortoises, and terrapins are animals that have a shell. The top portion is called the carapace; the abdominal shell is the plastron. Turtles may live in water or on land. Some, such as the box turtles, are able to close their shells protectively by closing portions of the hinged plastron to cover the vital head area and the rear legs and tail completely. All turtles have a major point in common. They have webbed feet, and both the front legs and the back legs are shaped for swimming.

A terrapin is one of a group of aquatic turtles that is found in the salt and brackish waters along the east coast and the Gulf coast into Texas. This group of turtles has the unfortunate characteristic to taste good when cooked. Combined into one genus, *Malaclemys*, this group has been hunted, captured, and killed as a food animal. Happily for the terrapins, this practice is much less widespread than it was in the past.

Tortoises are land animals. While at first appearance they look like turtles, there are several obvious differences. The most important physical difference is the shape of their legs and feet. Tortoises have short stumpy legs, not swimming legs. The forelegs are adapted for digging, while the back feet are blunt and stumpy, like those of a miniature elephant. Tortoises do not swim well, and frequently will drown if they get into water deeper than their shell. Tortoises have high domed shells and are frequently found in dry desert areas where no turtle would ever venture.

While there are differences, there is still enough similarity to consider the care of turtles and tortoises at the same time. In fact, we shall consider the care of aquatic turtles, those that live primarily in the water, as one group and land turtles and tortoises as another group.

One group of aquatic turtles we shall not consider is the soft-shell turtle and the snapping turtle. These turtles do not become tame, are uniformly unpredictable, and will lash out and bite without warning. They are dangerous. A saucer-sized snapper or soft-shell turtle can inflict a serious bite injury. They cannot be considered pets and have no place in a home aquarium.

At one time great numbers of aquatic turtles were sold from variety stores and pet shops. As many as 13 million were sold as pets in a single year. They were purchased as casually as greeting cards and bestowed on children who had no idea of how to care for them. Most of the baby turtles died quickly. Others lingered for periods of time on substandard diets and in unhealthy environments.

Then, because many of these turtles raised for sale were kept in unsanitary conditions, great numbers became infected with a bacterial organism called *Salmonella*. Since this organism is capable of infecting people, the sale of turtles became a public health issue. Eventually the commercial sale of turtles was stopped in most states, because those people raising and selling turtles would not correct the *Salmonella* situation. This is good: it prevented the needless death of millions of turtles.

You will want to take the best possible care of an individual turtle in your care, because you like turtles and have an interest in them.

Handling

We acquire most of our turtles and tortoises as injured specimens found along the highway. We repair the damage as best we can and offer care and security until the creature can care for itself. You may find a young turtle or tortoise and wish to try to raise it. An aquatic specimen of less than four inches (10 cm) in diameter is most adaptable to captivity and most likely to be raised. A land turtle this size would be an adult and will not adapt well and should not be taken from its habitat. If you do decide to take on this responsibility, be certain of several points.

In many states there are a variety of turtles and tortoises that are classed as threatened or endangered. These may not be kept or molested in any way. You must be sure the specimen you have found does not fall into this classification.

Obviously you will have a better chance of raising your turtle if you select a healthy specimen. A healthy turtle lifts its body off the ground when it walks. It has a smooth clean skin and shell with no discolored areas or soft spots.

Normally a turtle is picked up by grasping the right and left sides of its shell with your fingers and lifting it. Remember a soft-shell turtle and some snappers have long necks and can reach back and bite your fingers at that spot.

The soft hiss you may hear as you grasp the turtle is not a threat, but the air is being displaced from the lungs as the legs and head are drawn into the shell compressing the organs of the body.

A turtle or tortoise can be carried by the shell until you can find a cardboard box or other container to confine it while your terrarium is prepared.

Housing

Depending on your specimen, prepare a semiaquatic, woodland, or desert terrarium. Obviously your terrarium should contain plants, leaves, and other materials that are a part of the natural environment where your turtle lived. The shore of every stream or pond has all the plants and vegetation required to make your turtle feel at home.

An aquatic turtle less than four inches (10 cm) in diameter will do fine in a ten gallon (40 liter) aquarium. As we have said before, a larger size is better, for it's hard ever to have the home for your creature too big. (But one too small can definitely be harmful.)

Read the section on preparing the semiaquatic terrarium in the chapter on frogs, toads, and salamanders. The semiaquatic

An aquarium, a rock to crawl out on, and a siphon to change the water are all the equipment necessary to keep a turtle.

Red-eared turtle rests at the bottom of its aquarium.

terrarium for turtles is prepared the same way. However, for an aquatic turtle it would be better to position the plate glass divider so that at least two-thirds of the total area is water habitat.

Most aquatic turtles feed or eat in the water. The water in your terrarium must be deep enough for your turtle to maneuver about in, exercise in, and rest in, yet have shallow areas for basking. Water plants should be planted along the back edge and in the corners where they provide a natural appearance without blocking the water area for swimming.

A log or rock should be provided for the turtle to crawl out on to loaf.

All turtles require sunlight. The terrarium must be placed where it receives direct sunlight for a short period each day. The ideal temperature for the water in your terrarium is 75° to

Barking tree frog and aquatic turtle in their semiaquatic terrarium.

85°F (24°–29°C). While some sunlight is required, the terrarium should not be placed where the water overheats, or your turtle will certainly die. Place a thermometer partially in the water and monitor it carefully.

The water should be changed weekly by using a siphon. The waste water may be used to fertilize shrubbery or other plants. The clean water should ideally be dechlorinated, but from a practical standpoint we have never found this to be necessary for our turtles.

In preparing a woodland or desert terrarium, follow the directions given in the chapter on frogs, toads, and salamanders, also. The water bowl must be large enough for the land turtle to cover its shell completely with water. In addition, if a bowl is used, the sides must be modified by gluing bits of wood or rocks to them to make a firm footing so that the ungainly land turtle or tortoise can get out of the water easily.

Turtles and tortoises drink by immersing their mouths in water and sucking it up. The water in their bowl should be kept clean and changed regularly, so it is suitable and sanitary for drinking. If your turtle or tortoise is a frequent bather, you will have to change the water more frequently. If it seldom enters the water, changing it once a week should be adequate.

The temperature of the woodland terrarium should be 70° to 80°F (21°–27°C) for turtles and 75° to 85°F (24°–29°C) for tortoises.

For tortoises it is a good idea to suspend a 60-watt bulb slightly above ground level in one corner of the terrarium. You may plug it into a timer so it is on for about ten to twelve hours daily. Your tortoise will move close to the warmth of this bulb when it is chilly.

The land turtles and tortoises also require sunlight if they are to remain healthy. Either place the terrarium where it receives an hour of sunlight daily, or use a gro-light fluorescent tube that has light wave lengths as sunlight for four or five hours daily. A gro-light will provide the ultra violet radiation your turtle needs to activate the Vitamin D in its body and also will help your plants grow better.

An eastern box turtle in its woodland terrarium.

Feeding

A turtle feeds by grasping food in its jaws and breaking off the excess by pushing any outside the mouth with its front feet. This breaks off a bite-size portion which is swallowed.

An aquatic turtle is *carnivorous* or *omnivorous*. In captivity it will feed on bits of meat, liver, lettuce, or canned dog food dropped into the water. We feed our aquatic turtles bits of dry Purina Cat Chow. We break the dried food into bite-size or quarter pieces and drop them on the water.

Most turtles learn to eat quickly. When they become accustomed to people, they rise to the surface in anticipation when you approach the tank. A few will swallow the bits of Cat Chow while it is still floating, but most allow it to take on water, and as it sinks they swim up and swallow the softened piece. While it is said that you need not feed turtles but twice a week, ours have always preferred to eat every day. When it has eaten enough, the turtle will refuse further food offered.

The dried ant eggs sold as turtle food by pet shops are not an adequate diet for any turtle. Turtles must be offered a much more balanced diet if they are to be healthy.

In the wild, tortoises and land turtles eat primarily vegetable materials. In captivity they seem to relish and do better if they are offered animal protein, such as moistened cat or dog food. In addition, they will eat such things as spinach, lettuce, swiss chard, grapes, bananas, dandelion leaves, alfalfa hay bits, ground meat, earthworms, mixed frozen vegetables such as corn, peas, and lima beans, citrus fruit, and all leafy vegetables. Offer any foods you feel might tempt their appetites.

A favorite food to offer to get a land turtle started eating is strawberries. And few tortoises will resist bits of cantaloupe. If after a week you haven't convinced your land turtle or tortoise to eat, it is time to set it free. Most young animals adapt well, learn to eat, and look forward to feeding time, but some never adapt. It is far better to set an individual free before it becomes weak from malnutrition. Be certain you free it in exactly the same type of habitat as you found it.

Most tortoises adapt well to captivity. Some learn to come when called, and one tortoise even learned to come to the refrigerator each day at feeding time. Each is an individual and must be treated that way.

Once-a-day feeding and proper care of a natural habitat is not too much responsibility to expect if you are to have one of these fascinating creatures live at your home.

Breeding

Female turtles normally crawl out on land to lay their eggs in late spring or early summer. They choose the spot that suits them and then purposefully begin digging a hole with their back feet.

Each foot works alternately to scoop out the dirt until a four-to-five-inch-deep (10–12.5 cm) hole has been excavated. A dozen or more round soft-shelled eggs roll into the hole as the female rests with her rear quarters over the hole. When she is finished laying, she begins covering the eggs with loose dirt using her back feet.

From this point on, the embryo turtles are on their own. Sunlight warming the ground incubates the eggs. How long it takes before they hatch is determined by the temperature of the ground. When incubation is complete, a baby turtle uses an egg tooth on its nose to break open the leathery shell of the egg. Then it must struggle up through the sandy covering and make its way to the water.

Predation is heavy on both eggs and baby turtles. Raccoons and skunks find and feed on the eggs, while herons, raccoons, and other turtles feed on the newborn babies. But enough young survive to carry another generation into the future, as they have done for thousands of years.

If you are going to try to raise young turtles, you must have larger accommodations than the minimum-sized ten gallon aquarium. You must provide a habitat that will be large enough for a pair of adults and will make them feel secure in natural surroundings. Then when the urge to mate and lay eggs begins to stimulate the pair, this basic instinct will not be repressed by the stress of artificial confinement.

There are several important things you must do if you are going to try to hatch turtle eggs. Mark a *T* for top on the top-side of each egg with a felt-tipped pen. Turtle eggs must not be rotated from the position in which they are found. When the egg is moved, it should be done gently, always keeping the *T* topmost.

Mix one part peat moss and two parts sandy loam soil with water to a damp consistency, and use it to fill a large clay flower pot. Dig a hole in the soil mixture and place the eggs *T*-side up two inches (5 cm) deep in the dampened soil. Cover them gently.

Now place the pot with a thermometer in a clear plastic bag, seal it with a twist tie, and place it in subdued light at a temperature of 80° to 85°F (27°–29°C). Monitor the temperature daily while you wait for your eggs to hatch. After the eggs hatch, move the babies to a terrarium of the proper size and type.

In most species of turtles you can tell the difference between the males and females. The aquatic male turtles usually have longer, heavier tails than the females, and the claws on their front feet are usually a great deal longer. Many times, however, the female will be the larger in overall size.

Among the eastern box turtles most adult males have a bright red iris that makes the entire eye look red. This eye color is most noticeable during the breeding season of late spring and early summer. The eyes of the female box turtle are light brown in color.

Among the tortoises the males have longer, heavier tails than the females, and the plastron is rather concave.

Little is known of the courtship habits, breeding, interval before laying, incubation, and rate of growth of most turtles and tortoises. If you embark on a long-term project of attempting to breed and raise baby turtles, make certain you record all points you notice in the behavior of these individuals. Isolated facts and dates may begin to show a pattern over a period of time if you are observant.

Confinement of any wild creature should serve a useful purpose. It should expand our knowledge of their life history and not be just for our own amusement.

Diseases

Leeches: These external parasites frequently are found in wild turtles that are caught. They appear as flat black rounded organisms firmly attached to the soft skin of the turtle.

They may be pulled off if there are only one or two, but sometimes this damages the skin. If there are more than just a few, they may be induced to release their hold by applying vinegar or alcohol directly to the leeches with a cotton swab.

Shell Fractures: We obtain most of our turtles as injured animals. These slow-moving creatures are frequently injured as they cross a highway. Sometimes the shell is so badly damaged that the internal organs have also been crushed. We cannot help these except to stop further suffering through euthanasia.

But many have a cracked carapace or a piece broken out. These fractures we attempt to repair. We usually use Devco Five Minute Epoxy Glue or other quick drying cement to cement cracked shells together. Larger wounds or breaks are covered with a patch. Plastic, from a plastic milk jug, is flexible and makes good repair material. These patches are made slightly larger than the injured area and are cemented in place and allowed to remain attached to the shell as long as they will stay.

If the turtle will eat for us, we keep it for several weeks. We want to be certain it can fend for itself. If it is an adult turtle and will not eat in captivity, we turn it loose in a protected lake as soon as it appears to be able to crawl and swim normally.

Vitamin A Deficiency: This is a common nutritional deficiency seen frequently by veterinarians. The turtle has puffy swollen eyelids and a nasal discharge. If not treated, this condition progresses to a respiratory infection and pneumonia.

A vitamin A deficiency can be treated by adding oral vitamin drops containing A or a drop or two of cod liver oil to all food offered. If your turtle is cooperative, you can place a drop of multivitamins in its mouth daily. If the disease is more severe and has been allowed to go on for some time, the turtle should receive an injection of vitamins A, D, E from your veterinarian.

Vitamin D Deficiency: This condition frequently occurs along with vitamin A deficiency. It is seen commonly when turtles are not allowed some direct sunlight regularly. Turtles with this deficiency are depressed, don't eat well, and have enlarged leg joints. In prolonged deficiencies, the shell is deformed.

Treatment consists of placing your terrarium where the turtle receives exposure to direct sunlight for an hour or two each day and giving vitamin D orally. One or two drops of cod liver oil or a multiple vitamin supplement should be given with a dropper orally each day. However, do not overdose. Excessive cod liver oil can cause disease also.

Iodine Deficiency: Iodine deficiency occurs sometimes in captive turtles and tortoises. A lack of iodine causes enlargement of the thyroid glands which appears as swelling on the underside of the base of the neck. To prevent this from occurring, add a small amount of iodine to the drinking water. Obtain several ounces of a 10 percent Lugol's Solution from the drugstore. Add one drop of this solution to each cup of drinking water two to three times weekly.

SCUD (Ulcerative Shell Disease): This is an infectious ulceration of the shell of aquatic turtles. It is believed to be caused by a Proteus organism, which is a bacteria. Usually there are several spots where a dark discoloration appears on the shell, and the outer layer or plates appear to be coming loose or peeling off. The turtle will stop eating, becoming very droopy and lethargic as the infection spreads through its body. Then it becomes paralyzed and finally dies.

Start treatment when the first discolored spots on the shell are seen. Change the water and clean the terrarium. Provide more land and a rock or log where the turtle can get out of the water and bask. Place the terrarium where your turtle can receive several hours of sunlight daily, or place a grow lamp fluorescent bulb over the terrarium. These bulbs provide broad spectrum wave lengths of light similar to those of sunlight.

Place a thermometer in the terrarium and use a heat lamp or bulb to be certain the temperature remains between 80° and 85°F (27°–29°C).

Treat individual spots on the shell by applying an iodine solution on a Q-tip or cotton swab twice daily. Do not remove any loose portions of plates or the shell, but scrape off any loose crumbly portion with your iodine-saturated swab.

Be certain your turtle is eating a proper diet. Green leafy vegetables, green peas, dry Cat Chow bits, and bits of liver are well accepted by most turtles.

Injectable antibiotics, such as chloramphenicol and gentocin, can be given by your veterinarian daily for three or four days. This is necessary to prevent death if the disease has been going on for several days before you discover it.

Respiratory Disease; Pneumonia: Turtles on a deficient diet are more susceptible to respiratory infections and pneumonia. Turtles affected show a nasal discharge and bubbles from the nose on expiration, and they hold their mouths open to breathe. In the water they swim and float lopsided, with one side of the shell deeper than the other.

Treatment requires immediate action. Since the underlying cause is poor nutrition, stress, and exposure to bacteria such as *Aeromonas* and *Pseudomonas*, treatment includes needed environmental changes, nutritional changes, and specific treatment with an antibiotic.

The entire terrarium should be placed near a source of heat that will raise and keep the temperature of the water and air between 80° and 85°F (27°–29°C). The water in the tank should be changed every two days during the next three weeks. Be certain that the turtle receives direct sunlight for an hour or two every day or provide artificial sunlight with a grow light.

Bite-sized bits of fresh citrus fruit and hard-boiled egg yolk should be offered in addition to the other foods, such as leafy vegetables, Cat Chow bits, and liver bits, which are offered at least once daily. Any other foods your turtle likes to eat should be coated or injected with a vitamin supplement before it is offered.

If the turtle or tortoise is not eating, it must receive vitamins A, D, and C by injection, along with an injectable antibiotic—chloramphenicol or tetracycline. The turtle must be weighed to determine the proper dose of medication. Since half of the turtle's weight is shell, we give 25 mg of antibiotic per pound (55 mg per kg) of total body weight to achieve the proper amount of antibiotic. Ideally this daily amount is divided into two injections given twelve hours apart. From a practical standpoint your veterinarian may give all the medication in one injection each day. Normally the medication is given in the muscles of the rear leg just to one side or the other of the tail.

Enteritis: This is an intestinal infection. The turtle passes loose, bloody bowel material. This is not seen as frequently as respiratory disease, but it sometimes occurs in conjunction with that disease.

The treatment is exactly as for respiratory disease.

Mouth Rot: This is another disease considered to be related to poor nutrition and terrarium environment. Mouth rot is caused by a bacterial organism *Aeromonas hydrophila*. The turtle's mouth appears to be full of a yellow-gray crumbly exudate.

If you can handle and work with your turtle without causing further stress through struggling, use a cotton swab dipped in hydrogen peroxide to wipe out all the rotten exudate material. Then at least four times a day place a drop of a tetracycline solution in the mouth. We use Panmycin, a veterinary pediatric preparation made by the Upjohn Company, because it contains a high concentration of the antibiotic (100 mg per ml) in each drop.

In addition, vitamins A, D, and C and the antibiotic tetracycline or chloromycetin are given by injection each day for about four days.

All the management and feeding instructions given in respiratory infection treatment apply here also.

Since most of the infectious diseases veterinarians see are related to dietary deficiencies and poor management, you can prevent most diseases by proper care of your turtle.

Keep the water area clean. It is easy to change the water twice weekly using a siphon made for that purpose. This removes waste material eliminated by your turtle and decaying food that won't be eaten.

Be certain your turtles receive direct sunlight regularly, or set up an incandescent grow lamp that provides the wave lengths of sunlight. This is necessary for proper utilization of vitamin D in your turtle's body and helps control other problems. Turtles enjoy basking in the warmth of these lights or sunlight.

For proper digestion and enzyme function in your turtle's body, it must have warmth. Be certain it can bask where the temperature is 80° to 85°F (27°–29°C) or provide an incandescent lamp that will keep the temperature at that range somewhere in your terrarium. While this warmth is important, overheating by keeping it in the sun too long or not monitoring the temperature with a thermometer is even worse. A turtle or tortoise will die quickly if it gets too hot.

If you can get your turtle eating a balanced diet along with this proper management, you will seldom see the infectious diseases mentioned here.

While turtles and tortoises are considered to be unfeeling chelonians, there is no doubt in my mind that their health is dependent on affectionate care, in a place where they feel safe and secure, by a compassionate owner who knows their requirements.

References and Suggested Reading

Dolensak, E. P., and Barbara Burn. *A Practical Guide to Impractical Pets*. New York: Viking Press, 1976.

Frye, Fredric L. *Husbandry, Medicine, and Surgery in Captive Reptiles*. Bonner Springs, Kans.: Veterinary Medicine Publishing Co., 1973.

Tulodziecki, Norman. *Reptile Medicine Notes*. Columbus: Ohio State University, College of Veterinary Medicine, 1976.

11 / Snakes and Lizards

Snakes are fascinating to many people and surprisingly popular as pets. Lizards, too, have many loyal supporters. Lizards and snakes are part of the same order, Squamata; and in fact, many consider snakes to be legless lizards. Because of their similarities, snakes and lizards will be considered together in this chapter.

Choose any one of the docile native species of North American snakes for a pet. Under no circumstances should you consider one of the poisonous species. The garter snake makes a good pet and is found in most areas of the country. King snakes, corn snakes, and yellow rat snakes are popular, too. Most of these varieties tame down and adapt well to captivity.

While the average survival time for a snake in a zoological exhibit or zoo is two years, most species have the potential to live for ten to fifteen years. Snakes and lizards that are well cared for, provided with proper food, and whose unique specific requirements are catered to not only live for their expected life span but reproduce in captivity.

While there are a number of different species of snakes in North America, they have common characteristics. All snakes shed their skin two to six times yearly. All snakes have no eyelids, but they do have a layer of clear skin that covers and protects the eye. This eye cover, or spectacle, is shed when the snake sheds its skin. A snake has no ear openings, but all snakes detect vibrations through their entire body. Among the nonpoisonous snakes, the flicking tongue is the most important sense organ in finding food. Tiny airborne particles adhere to the moist tongue and are carried to an area in the roof of the mouth. These scent particles identify potential food for the snake, for snakes hunt by scent rather than sight.

Poisonous snakes, such as rattlesnakes and moccasins, have small facial pits between the nose and the eyes that are heat receptors. These pits are sensitive to the radiant body heat given off by the small mammals that are the primary prey of these snakes. The pits are used to identify poisonous snakes in the group known as pit vipers.

The only two species of lizards considered poisonous are the Gila monster and the Mexican beaded lizard. Many of the other two hundred species of lizards found in North America make good pets. You must learn about the life history and food habits of your particular species if you are going to provide the quality of care that will allow your lizard to live a long, contended, healthy life.

Lizards vary in size from those about three inches (7–10 cm) long to those over three feet (1 meter) in length. Lizards are found in all types of habitats from wet swampland to high desert. Their habits and food preferences depend on the habitat in which they live.

The lizard most commonly kept as a pet is the Carolina anole. Many people call them chameleons because of their ability to change skin color from green to light tan, but this is not the correct name for this small lizard from the South.

Both lizards and snakes vary considerably in their ability to

adapt to captivity and to humans. If the specimen you have
selected is unruly, bites, and spends most of its time attempting
to escape. I would suggest you turn it loose in its normal habitat, or where you captured it, and try another specimen. Certainly if you are unable to get the creature to eat, or you are
unable to supply proper food, you must free it before it gets
too weak to fend for itself.

Handling

Everyone is fearful handling a snake for the first time. The
snake is frightened, too. Even when you are gentle, a terrified
snake that has not been handled may bite as a means of self-
defense.

Until the snake finds out that you don't intend to hurt it and
that the warmth of your hands is pleasurable, it would be best
to wear soft leather gloves. The bite of a nonpoisonous snake is
seldom very painful unless you panic and jerk your hand away.
A snake has several rows of short, sharp teeth that point in the
direction of the throat. If you jerk your hand free, it's like pulling against a whole group of tiny sharp thorns, and your skin
may tear.

If you are bitten you must be calm. Place the snake's body
on a table, in the cage, or on the floor so it has some support.
Then if the snake doesn't turn loose at once, place the thumb
of your free hand on one side of the snake's face just below the
eye and the index finger on the other side of the head, opposite
your thumb, and gently squeeze the finger and the thumb together, forcing the jaws open.

When the jaws open, free your skin gently from the snake's
teeth, place the snake back in the cage, and then wash any
wound thoroughly and apply a suitable antiseptic.

Actually, if you wear gloves the first couple of times you
handle your snake, there is little danger. Snakes usually find
they aren't going to be hurt, and don't struggle or bite after
the second or third time they are handled. A snake that is persistent in its efforts to bite and escape should be set free. It is

A young nonpoisonous snake is easy to handle.

better to try again with a better-dispositioned and more even-tempered individual than to have to put up with an unruly rowdy.

When your snake does not attempt to bite, after the third or fourth session of handling, discard the gloves. Always support the snake's body with one or both hands. When it feels supported and secure, it will usually rest quietly.

It is best to pick up a snake by grasping it gently around the body just behind the head. That way you control the head and can restrain the snake if it starts to take off. Slide your other hand under the main portion of the snake's body and lift. Move slowly and gently as you bring the snake's body up close to your own. Most snakes enjoy the warmth that radiates from your body and are content to be carried about for hours.

Lizards, too, become accustomed to handling. With one hand, grasp a small lizard around its body to lift it—never by the tail. Lizards are very quick and agile. Until they become accustomed to you, they may leap and escape in a split second.

If you grasp many of the smaller lizards by the tail, you probably will end up holding just a tail, for many lizards' tails come off at the slightest provocation. This is a means of defense for them. While the predator is occupied with the tail, its owner makes its escape. The lizard can grow another tail, but that takes time.

Lizards also bite in defense and in fright. They, too, have several rows of tiny sharp teeth. The shock of being bitten is far worse than the slight pain. They are so quick they grab you, bite down, and release before you have time to react.

Some of the larger lizards can inflict considerable damage with their bite and should not be handled unless they are accustomed to you and have proven themselves trustworthy.

If you must transport a lizard any distance, it is best to place it in a cloth bag or pillow case with the open end tied securely. If it does escape, don't chase it, but just watch it. It is almost impossible to catch a small lizard when it is moving. They are too fast and quickly evade our clumsy grasp.

Wait for it to become quiet and still. It will usually stay in that spot. Make a loop of nylon thread or fishing line to use as a snare. Use a slip knot that will pull tight and fashion the loop large enough to slip easily over the lizard's head. Attach the loop to a fishing pole or a stick about three feet (1 meter) long. Gently work the noose over the lizard's head and tighten it when it is around the neck area. Quickly lift the lizard to its cage, or cloth bag, and remove the snare.

While some lizards become quite docile, some even to the point of stretching out their necks to have their chins scratched or stroked, or eating tidbits from your fingers, most are hard to catch if they get loose. Since your interest is primarily in studying their behavior, confine your handling to your specimen in its terrarium.

Housing

Snakes and lizards do quite well in semiaquatic or woodland terrariums prepared as discussed in the chapter on frogs, toads, and salamanders. A ten gallon (40 liter) aquarium would be large enough for only the smallest snake or one or two small lizards. A larger living area for even these small creatures would be better.

You can make a good terrarium. Build a framework of wood. The bottom should be of half-inch exterior plywood and have solid sides of boards part way up to retain the gravel, charcoal, and soil of your terrarium. Give the base several coats of good exterior paint so it will be waterproof. Install a piece of plate glass for the front so you can see your specimen. The back wall can be solid boards painted to blend into the woodland scene. The two ends should have areas of window screen to provide good ventilation. A well-fitting top of small-mesh hardware-cloth or wood-framed window screen may be hinged to the back side. The hinged top provides good access to the entire terrarium.

Be sure the top fits well on whatever type of cage you make, for a snake can slide through the smallest opening. I have lost three snakes in our house at different times. Our house is open to the porch much of the time, and the snakes must have escaped from the house to the porch to the outside, for we have never found any one of the three. Your family may not be as understanding as my wife is, even though she dislikes snakes; so be certain you have an escapeproof home for your specimen.

The cage or terrarium should be at least as long as the snake will be when it is full grown, and at least half as wide as it is long. The height should be as tall as the terrarium is wide.

While newspapers are easy to clean and make a satisfactory floor for your cage, I prefer the more natural-appearing terrarium with woodland plants and materials from where your captive normally lives.

Plants may be left in their pots in the terrarium soil. That way each plant can be watered to its individual needs.

A bathing and drinking pond can be prepared by sinking a large bowl or metal cake pan in the soil up to its rim. Artfully planted, the water can appear as a small pond in your terrar-

The Carolina anole stakes out its territory in the terrarium.

ium. It must be large enough for the snake to crawl into and immerse itself.

A piece of a log, some leaves, and several large rocks to form a cave add variety to your terrarium and offer a sanctuary where your snake or lizard can hide. Since many snakes, and practically all lizards, climb, several good-size branches should be placed in one corner and along the back part of the cage to offer a variety of perches.

Since lizards usually establish vertical territories, there must be several branches if you have more than one lizard in the terrarium. Each lizard will claim its branch and defend it from ground level to the topmost tip of the branches. A snake uses the branches for climbing, but also it will rub against them to help loosen the skin at shedding time.

Since snakes and lizards are cold-blooded (ectotherms), they require warmth from outside their bodies. Each reptile has a "preferred optimal temperature" (POT). This POT must be reached each day if the normal body functions, such as digestion and elimination, are to take place. For most reptiles this temperature is between 68° and 103°F (20°–39°C).

In nature the snake or lizard will bask in the sun until its body reaches the preferred optimal temperature (POT). Then as the digestive enzymes begin working on the food it has eaten and digestion is taking place, the snake or lizard will move into a cool shady spot. In your terrarium you must simulate nature by providing both a warm basking spot and cooler shady spots for your specimen. You may provide a warm spot in the cage by placing a heating pad under one corner of the cage. Set it on low and just keep this spot warm and available at all times. The heating pad must not heat the entire cage, and you must be certain it is not overheating, which could cause damage or fire. I prefer to provide a basking spot by hanging a 60-watt bulb in a shielded housing at one side of the cage. This close-fitting metal shade will focus the warmth on the floor of the terrarium in one spot. The light may be placed on a timer, so that for five to six hours each day there is a warm basking area available. You can just turn it on and off manually each day, but the timer is more consistent.

An incandescent light in a shield reflector makes a good basking light.

Basking is an effective way of soaking up radiant heat. Your lizards and snakes will move into the spot of warmth, soak up the heat they need, and then retreat to a cooler spot. It is essential that different temperature gradients be available in the terrarium. That way the creature can choose the amount of warmth it needs and the temperature it finds most comfortable. It has been found that a reptile kept at its preferred optimal temperature all the time will not live long, and a temperature one or two degrees warmer than the POT is quickly fatal. Since it is impossible to control the temperature in the terrarium to such close tolerances, let the animal do it for you.

We also know that snakes and lizards must have sunshine. This can be provided by placing your terrarium where the direct sunlight can pass through the screened top for an hour or two each day. Or you can use a grow lamp, which provides the full spectrum of light rays from a fluorescent bulb. One of the primary reasons for putting a screened top on your cage or terrarium is to be able to position your fluorescent light just above the cage, so that the entire area is bathed in broad spectrum rays. Snakes like to sun themselves under these lights. It was found that some snakes that were starving themselves to death in zoological exhibits began to eat when they were allowed exposure to this type of fluorescent light. These lights are also beneficial to your plants by making them grow well. These broad spectrum lights should be kept on for fourteen hours each day.

Ultraviolet lights should not be used. These can cause permanent eye damage, skin damage, and even death. While the wide spectrum fluorescents do produce ultraviolet rays, these rays make up a very small, but necessary, percentage of the total light output.

A thermometer in your terrarium is a must. A hygrometer, an instrument to measure relative humidity, along with the thermometer is ideal. A terrarium temperature that fluctuates between 65° and 85°F (18°–29°C), with a basking spot where the temperature is higher, is ideal. A relative humidity of 50 to 70 percent is also the ideal to strive for. You can regulate the humidity by using a mist sprayer to water the plants, vegetation, and ground in your terrarium.

In nature the snake or lizard will seek warmth several times a day. It basks and then seeks shade to rest. If the temperature falls below the point where your cold-blooded friend functions well, it becomes torpid. Its metabolic rate goes to almost zero, and it goes into hibernation until the environmental temperature rises again.

While it is good to offer the temperature gradients in your terrarium and provide the essential wide spectrum light required, it is best not to let the temperature fall to the low levels that force hibernation.

Ecdysis (Shedding of Skin)

A snake's skin is a series of scales. Each scale is attached at the front edge and elevated at the back edge. The outer elevated portion, or epidermal portion, is the part that is shed.

The clear portion of skin covering the eyes is called the spectacle. This covering is normally clear. Seven to fourteen days before the actual shedding takes place, the spectacle becomes

Appearance of spectacle over the eye prior to shedding.

cloudy and then very gray and opaque. The snake is essentially blind at this time. At this same time the colors of the skin are dull and muddy.

As the old skin begins to loosen, the spectacle begins to clear. The skin colors look brighter again. Several days after the eye once again becomes clear, the snake will shed.

A young growing snake will shed every five or six weeks. An adult snake sheds two to four times a year. Not all snakes have an easy time getting rid of this old skin.

It helps to keep the relative humidity around 70 percent when you know shedding is taking place. It helps to have water where the snake can completely immerse its body to soften and loosen the skin. Snakes can drown, so the water should not be deep, and certainly you should not force it to stay in the water.

You might provide sticks, branches, and rocks for your snake to rub against. This helps loosen the skin, and the rubbing scrapes the skin off the snake's body.

It helps to provide a quiet sanctuary after shedding, for the brightly colored new skin is soft and tender. If the snake is forced to move about, the new skin will be damaged and will look rough, dull, and crusty until the next time the snake sheds.

Even though you provide all the essentials to make it easy for your snake to shed, sometimes it doesn't. You may have to help. If your snake hasn't shed a week after the spectacle clears, soak its body in a shallow pan of water for ten minutes about three times during the day. You may spray your snake with your mist water sprayer several times a day. Then try gently to remove the patches of dead skin.

If the spectacles do not clear and the skin has already been shed, they may have to be removed. Gently apply water to these spectacles several times during the day with a mist sprayer. When the spectacles appear to be soft, gently rub around the edge with a moistened cotton swab until you see an edge beginning to loosen and becoming free. Concentrate on this spot. Moisten the spectacle repeatedly and gradually peel the dead covering off the eye. Don't rub the new tissue under the spectacle any more than you can help. Work at peeling the edge of the old covering back until you finally have it completely removed. If you are not sure what you are doing, ask your veterinarian for help.

A snake will not eat during the shedding process. Once it is finished and the new skin has become dry and firm, your snake will usually be hungry and ready to eat.

Feeding

Snakes have four to six rows of teeth that hold the food they grasp. They have a stretchable, mobile lower jaw that facilitates swallowing of large food items. A snake can normally swallow an object at least as large as its head. What your snake or lizard eats depends on the species and to some degree on what it is used to eating in its natural habitat.

As you know, the tongue is the snake's most important sense organ for finding food. In nature most nonpoisonous snakes feed on salamanders, smaller snakes, mice, rats, birds and bird eggs, frogs and toads, crickets and other insects, and all types of worms.

Most of the smaller snakes that eat earthworms, crickets, and other insects prefer to eat every day. Larger snakes that feed on mammals and larger prey may eat only every other week. Lizards eat daily.

All snakes are considered to be carnivores. Small snakes feed on whatever moving prey they can find that is smaller than they are. You may offer meal worms, earthworms (see chapter on frogs, toads, and salamanders, for information on keeping earthworms), crickets, and any other crawling insects you can find.

Larger snakes are frequently fed mice, rats, frogs, and toads. I guess I like mice, frogs, and toads too much ever to offer them as food to another creature.

I greatly admire the boy author Ronald Rood tells about in his book *May I Keep This Clam, Mother? It Followed Me Home.* Since snakes feed primarily by sense of smell, he tricked his hognose snake into eating a piece of beef by rubbing the meat against the toad's skin. He also fooled his garter snake by putting meat and his frog together, and putting the odor of a mouse on meat for his milk snake. Now, that's my kind of boy!

I just don't like the idea of killing one creature to feed another. I think it's great to use fresh road-killed birds or squirrels or other small mammals rather than let them go to waste, but I won't feed a mouse or a frog, killed for that purpose.

If you feed a mouse or rat to your snake, teach your snake to accept its food dead. You can stun these prey animals and offer them while they are warm and moving. When your snake accepts them this way, offer them dead. This is done for two reasons.

First, it is easier on the creature offered as food. In addition, every veterinarian who sees unusual pets has seen snakes that have been severely bitten by a mouse or rat. If the snake isn't hungry, it may become the victim when offered a live animal.

Don't handle larger snakes the day they are to be fed or handle them for several hours after eating. Many will refuse to eat if they are handled before eating, and some will vomit their food if you pick them up after they have eaten.

Garter snakes normally feed on earthworms, frogs, slugs, and crickets. They can be taught to eat canned dog food, hamburger supplemented with calcium and vitamins, and bits of fish supplemented with vitamins. Start by mixing earthworms into the food you want your garter snake to eat, so it will have the earthworm odor. As it learns to accept the food you prepare, gradually cut off the earthworms. Garter snakes, like most snakes, are most active at night, so feed them in the evening and leave the food in at night. The food should be in bite-size portions.

Larger snakes can be fed chunks of meat in which you have placed extra calcium and a multivitamin capsule. Larger snakes will eat whole eggs. If snakes eat too much, too often they will become fat. If they don't get enough to eat, they won't grow.

If your snake goes for four weeks without eating, it is in trouble. You must either let it go or start force-feeding it. If it is possible, force a piece of meat down the snake's throat with a blunt forceps. Then with your fingers, massage the chunk down into the stomach.

However, I prefer to pass a stomach tube and feed a liquid diet. There are a number of formulas that are used, but our basic diet is egg. This egg is stirred up well with a fork, and a half teaspoonful of a multiple vitamin powder is added to it along with an ounce (30 ml) of milk.

This food is placed in a plastic food dispenser of the type used to dispense catsup. For a three-foot (1 meter) boa we would use a stomach tube about a quarter of an inch (6 mm) in diameter and twelve to fourteen inches (30–35 mm) long. Gently force the snake's mouth open wide enough to admit the moistened tube. The stomach tube is inserted until the tip is about one-third into the length of the snake's body. This is where the stomach should be. The tip of the plastic dispenser containing the formula is inserted into the stomach tube. Gently and slowly the contents are expelled through the tube into the snake's stomach. Feed less to smaller snakes. After the animal has been fed, gently place it back in its cage where it can rest. Handling after feeding, or feeding too much, will cause the snake to vomit. If this does occur, allow it to rest quietly until the next day, then repeat the procedure using one-third less formula.

If the snake is sick we add antibiotics to the formula that we are giving. After the dispenser is empty the tube is slowly and gently removed.

We use this means of force-feeding for sick snakes primarily. If you have captured a snake and are obliged to feed it in this fashion, I would suggest that you turn it loose. Although some snakes have been maintained for years on force-feeding, I would rather have a more adaptable snake as a specimen—one that can learn to eat on its own.

All snakes don't want to eat during shedding. Most become slow, droopy, and won't eat if their terrarium temperature goes below 70°F (21°C). Many northern snakes will instinctively want to hibernate in fall and will not want to eat. By regulating the temperature and length of daylight, most of these snakes can be convinced that winter isn't coming after all.

Feeding a lizard is usually easier than feeding a snake. Most of the smaller lizards are insect eaters. The anoles, skinks, and fence lizards eat insects such as baby crickets, flies, mosquitoes, meal worms, and other small worms. Horned lizards of the Southwest primarily eat ants. The chuckwalla and crested lizard eat primarily fruit and vegetables. Iguanas are fed meal worms, earthworms, lettuce, flower blossoms, thawed frozen mixed vegetables, fresh fruit, and dog food. Other lizards can be taught to eat canned dog food, scrambled eggs, puppy chow, insects, worms, fruits, and other food supplemented with extra calcium and vitamins.

Read about what your lizard eats in the wild and then offer the foods you have available that most nearly meet its needs. When I have anoles, fence lizards, and skinks, I keep their aquarium out of doors. I use a fine-mesh hardware-cloth that allows flies, mosquitoes, and other small insects to enter the terrarium without allowing the lizard to leave. While I never keep them for more than a couple of weeks, these small lizards are able to obtain their own food while they stay with us.

Since a horned lizard feeds primarily on ants, you would have a difficult time trying to catch the number it needs each day. It is far easier to make a feeding cage that has a mesh bottom. Place this cage on or near an ant bed and let the lizard catch its own food. You must watch, however, that the ants don't attack your lizard. It can't flee and escape, so you must be watchful and protect it. If you live in the North you will have to start an ant farm or raise baby crickets to feed your horned lizard when the ground is frozen and covered with snow.

Lizards and snakes must have water available. Lizards drink by lapping up the water with their tongue. In the wild, small lizards, such as the anole, drink by licking at drops of water that collect on vegetation from the dew or rain. In your terrarium you must provide drinking water by spraying the vegetation with a mist sprayer each day.

Larger lizards will lap water from the water dish or pond in your terrarium.

Snakes drink by immersing their mouth in the water and sucking it up. Be certain the water in the miniature pond in your terrarium is clean and suitable for drinking. Change it regularly once a week, or more frequently if it doesn't appear clean.

Some lizards and small snakes like to bask after eating. While basking, their body temperature is elevated. This enhances digestion and frequently stimulates intestinal motility, and thus elimination. Lizards eliminate more frequently than snakes, which sometimes defecate only two or three times a month. The feces eliminated are usually semiliquid and smelly. As soon as they dry out they should be removed. Your terrarium should not just look nice, you want it to smell clean.

Breeding

In many species of snakes and lizards, it is difficult to tell the difference between males and females. Tails of male snakes generally are longer than females, from the tip to the vent (anal opening) and more tapered. A female's tail tends to be shorter and fatter. Some male lizards have distinctive patches of color that identify them for you, such as the blue patch under the necks of the skinks and fence lizards.

However, if you are interested in breeding snakes or lizards, you will either need the expert advice of a herpetologist, or you can create a habitat large enough to accommodate three or four individuals of the same species. The law of averages should provide a pair. However, male lizards are territorial and so are some snakes. They must have room to avoid each other or fighting will occur. The dominant lizard will intimidate the others and will not allow them to eat.

Snakes or lizards that lay eggs are called oviparous. These eggs are usually rather soft with white leathery shells. If you are going to try to hatch these eggs, you must control the temperature and the humidity around the eggs.

The best way to do this is to incubate them in a clear plastic or polyethylene bag. Select a quart-size bag for a few small eggs, and a gallon-size bag for larger eggs or a group of eggs. Hatch the eggs on sterile moist peat moss placed in the bag. The peat moss may be sterilized by placing it in a shallow pan in the oven set at 300°F (150°C) for an hour. After the peat moss has cooled down, add water to it until it is slightly damp but still fluffy. Fill the bag just half full of the damp peat moss.

The ideal incubation temperature is 85°F (29°C). Most eggs will tolerate temperatures that go ten F degrees (six C degrees) higher or lower than this, but try to maintain the temperature.

Place the plastic bag containing the peat moss in subdued light where it will stay during the forty-three-to-sixty-day incubation period. Nestle the eggs in the moss, so they are half covered, but where you can see them well. Fill the bag with as much air as you can get into it and seal the bag. Unless the eggs show signs of a problem, the bag may remain sealed throughout the incubation period. There will be enough oxygen trapped in the bag to supply the needs of the incubating eggs.

Check the eggs and the incubation temperature daily. A white fluffy coating on the eggs means a fungus is growing on them. This is a threat to the eggs. Open the incubation bag and wipe the eggs off with a soft cloth. Fungus growth usually means the moss is too damp. If it feels damp, allow some of the moisture to evaporate before you replace the eggs and reseal the bag.

If a dent appears in the soft shell of an egg during the first half of the incubation period, it means the moss is too dry and the eggs are drying out. Open the bag and spray a fine mist of water on the eggs and moss each day until the eggs take on enough moisture to become round again, then reseal the bag. Dents that appear late in incubation can be normal and the eggs should not be bothered.

The length of incubation depends on the type of egg, and is not known for a great many species. It is up to you to keep an accurate record of all phases of breeding, egg laying, incubation, and any other things you notice. Perhaps you can fill in some of the gaps in reptile knowledge as you hatch the eggs.

Some female snakes retain the eggs within their body for the entire incubation period, which may be as long as three months. The young snakes hatch in her body, or the female expels the eggs just as they are ready to hatch. This type of snake is called an ovoviviparous snake and includes some of the water snakes, pit vipers, and the garter snake.

It is easiest to select a nonpoisonous ovoviviparous snake that bears live young if you wish to breed snakes. That way there are no eggs to be concerned with, and the newborn snakes are able to care for themselves from birth. They must be protected from other larger snakes or they may be eaten.

The raising of baby snakes and lizards is a real challenge. Certainly it would be easier if you provided a habitat that simulated the natural environment. In addition it would be essential for you to provide the basics of proper humidity, temperatures, and an adequate diet. Succeeding in a project of this type would be far more stimulating than passively keeping an individual reptile captive.

Diseases

Rat Bite: Many small boas and other snakes large enough to be fed rats are frequently attacked by these mammals. Multiple wounds are found over the entire body. If the wounds are not severe, an antibiotic ointment applied to the wounds daily may be all that is necessary. In more severe cases, antibiotic injections should be given by your veterinarian to prevent infection.

This type of injury can be prevented by feeding only dead mice and rats.

Constipation: Snakes usually eliminate several times a month. A larger snake fed furry mammals over a period of time may have a fecal mass of fur and other indigestible material that it cannot eliminate. Treatment usually requires help from your veterinarian. He will infuse a lubricant material through the anus, give stool-softening agents with a stomach tube, or if necessary surgically remove the mass.

Tumors: Snakes also get tumors. If the tumor is in the abdominal area it may feel like a fecal mass. A tumor must be removed surgically after the proper diagnosis is made by your veterinarian.

Vomiting after Eating: If the snake's body temperature does not reach POT regularly, digestion cannot occur. The spoiled, undigested food may be vomited. Handling a snake soon after it has eaten may also trigger vomiting.

To prevent vomiting be certain your snake has the warmth for basking, and don't handle it after it has eaten.

Burns: If your warming light is too close to the snake's body, the snake may be burned. An unshielded incandescent bulb should not be used, but rather a light that focuses the warmth on the floor of the cage. Place a thermometer in the area of warmth and check the temperature periodically. It should be from 100°F to 105°F (38°–41°C) at the warmest spot where the snake or lizard may lie.

If the snake has been burned, apply a soothing antibacterial ointment, such as Panalog (Squibb), to the spot.

Calcium Deficiency: Frequently lizards and snakes fed a diet of insects and/or meat will become deficient in calcium. In calcium deficiency, fractures and deformed legs occur in lizards. A deformed spinal column is the most common sign in calcium-deficient snakes.

When your animal eats primarily insects, such as crickets, or pieces of beef or hamburger, it must receive supplemental calcium and vitamins A and D. Calcium gluconate or dicalcium phosphate capsules may be dissolved in the drinking water. These are not prescription drugs and may be obtained from your veterinarian, drugstore, or pet store. Vitamins may be given by placing a capsule in the piece of meat. Feed your lizard dog food, which is better balanced than meat, in addition to the insects.

Iodine Deficiency: Iodine deficiency is not as common as calcium deficiency, but it does occur in captive reptiles. A lack of iodine causes enlargement of the thyroid glands which appears as swelling on the underside of the base of the neck. To prevent this from occurring, add a small amount of iodine to the drinking water. Obtain several ounces of a 10 percent Lugol's Solution from the drugstore. Add one drop of this solution to each cup of drinking water two to three times weekly.

Mites and Ticks: Snake mites, *Ophionyssus natricis*, are seen as tiny gray dots that crawl between and under the free edge of the snake's scales. Mites are seen most frequently around the eye, the chin, and the vent. Mites are serious, for they suck blood. In large numbers mites seriously weaken a snake or lizard.

Ticks appear as brown spiderlike creatures attached to the snake's skin. Ticks are seen rather frequently in specimens caught in the wild.

Plastic strips impregnated with Vapona, such as the Shell pest strips, are used to kill both mites and ticks. A section of the strip two by four inches (5 × 10 cm) is placed on the wire top of the cage for twelve hours or overnight. The fumes will penetrate the entire cage and kill any insect present. This treatment should be repeated weekly for four weeks. Do not leave the strip on the cage all the time. The strips have been considered to be responsible for killing some smaller lizards when they were kept in their cages.

Internal Parasites (Worms): More than five hundred intestinal parasites have been found to affect reptiles. With such a variety of parasites, there are no specific symptoms nor any *single* effective treatment for all internal parasites.

A microscopic examination of the fecal material is necessary to make a diagnosis. Your veterinarian will make a direct smear examination and a flotation examination. If your snake or lizard has worms, the specific medication will be dispensed based on how much your snake or lizard weighs.

Normally tapeworms are treated with Niclosamide (Yomesan-Chemagro) at the rate of 75 mg per pound (165 mg per kg) of body weight. Nematodes, or roundworms, are usually treated with Thiabendazole (Merck) at the rate of 25 mg per pound (55 mg per kg) of body weight. Both of these substances may be added to food or given by stomach tube.

Amebiasis: This is a serious protozoan disease with the primary symptom of bloody diarrhea. It is treated with Metronidazole (Flagyl-Searle). This medication is given orally with a stomach tube at the rate of 100 mg per pound (200 mg per kg) of body weight.

Blister Disease: In this disease the snake or lizard has brownish fluid-filled blisters scattered over the skin. On the underside of the abdomen the lesions appear as flat brown spots under the scales. This is a bacterial infection and is associated with dirty, damp quarters.

The terrarium or cage should be thoroughly cleaned. The humidity must be monitored to see that it stays between 50 and 70 percent, and the temperature in the cage should be 80°F (27°C). Be sure you have a broad spectrum fluorescent light for the terrarium as well as a focused incandescent light where the snake can bask at its POT.

The individual spots should be treated with an iodine solution. If the snake is not eating, it should receive an injection of chloramphenicol to stop any internal extension of this skin infection.

SCUD-Ulcerative Stomatitis-Mouth Rot: This is a bacterial infection. There appear to be cheesy, grayish-white particles in the snake's mouth. The area around the teeth is red and the entire mouth is sore. The snake feels bad and will not eat.

Poor sanitation, unclean quarters, high humidity, and lack of vitamin C are all considered to be involved. This poor environment lowers the snake's resistance allowing the *Pseudomonas* or *Aeromonas* infection to get started. If untreated, the infection progresses to pneumonia and then death.

Treatment requires a three-fold approach. First, clean up and apply the environmental measures listed for blister disease.

Second, gently clean the mouth with cotton swabs moistened with hydrogen peroxide. Remove only the loose material; do not damage the tissues by trying to scrape the "crud" out of the mouth. Four times a day apply several drops of Panmycin (Upjohn) or Panalog(Squibb) to the lesions in the mouth.

Third, the snake should receive tetracycline or chloramphenicol and vitamin C daily either by injection or orally, for ten days. Use a stomach tube to give 50 mg per pound (100 mg per kg) of body weight of either antibiotic and 100 mg of vitamin C each day. Since you are using the stomach tube anyway, include some of the egg, milk, and vitamin formula (as given under feeding) to build the snake up. The amount of formula to give depends on the size of the snake, but a tablespoonful of formula per pound (33 cc per kg) of body weight daily would be beneficial.

Respiratory Infection: With this infection, the snake or lizard breathes with its mouth open, and sometimes blows bubbles from the mouth or nose. It is depressed, will not eat, and looks sick.

Treat the snake with the same threefold approach given under SCUD.

Snout Abrasions: A snake will sometimes rub its snout against the cage screen almost continuously while trying to escape. Cover the screens with soft cloth and treat the raw snout with an antibiotic ointment daily for several days. If the snake will not adapt to captivity, set it free.

Remember, whenever you feel you can't provide proper care or supply proper food, it is time to set your snake or lizard free. If it is to survive, this must be done before the creature becomes too weak to fend for itself. Free it in an environment that is familiar and normal for that animal.

References and Suggested Reading

Boever, W. J., and R. Houser. "Intestinal Parasitisms in Reptiles," *Modern Veterinary Practice*, April 1977, pp. 337–338.

Dolensek, E. P., and Barbara Burn. *A Practical Guide to Impractical Pets*. New York: Viking Press, 1976.

Frye, Fredric. *Husbandry, Medicine, and Surgery in Captive Reptiles*. Bonner Springs, Kans.: Veterinary Medicine Publishing Co., 1973.

Jacobson, E. R. "Histology, Endocrinology, and Husbandry of Ecdysis in Snakes," *VM/SAC*, February 1977, pp. 275–280.

Tulodzieck, Norman. *Reptile Medicine Notes*. Columbus: Ohio State University, College of Veterinary Medicine, 1976.

Wallach, Joel D. "Environmental and Nutritional Diseases of Captive Reptiles," *Journal of the American Veterinary Medical Association*, volume 159, no. 11, December 1, 1971, pp. 1632–1642.

Wallach, Joel D. "Management and Nutritional Problems in Captive Reptiles," *Current Veterinary Therapy*, vol. VI. Philadelphia: W. B. Saunders, 1977.

12 / Budgerigars (Parakeets), Canaries, and Parrots

There are more than 25 million pet birds in the United States. These include mynahs, canaries, and many others. The *psittacine* group of birds, which includes parrots, lories, lorikeets, cockatoos, cockatiels, macaws, and more than twenty different types of parakeets, makes up the majority.

The various species of parakeets all come from Africa, Asia, South America, Central America, and Australia. The common small pet parakeet, *Melopsittacus undulatus*, is one of these. It comes from Australia and is correctly called a budgerigar. Budgerigar is an Australian bush word that means "pretty bird." We will hereafter refer to them as budgies.

Budgies come in a variety of colors. The blues and greens are the most common, but there are yellows, white, cinnamon, and many others. They have strong legs for climbing, a malletlike tongue, and the hooked beak characteristic of all psittacine birds. Between the beak and the eyes is a band of tissue called the cere. The color of the cere is an aid in distinguishing between male and female birds.

In young budgies, the cere is a pale blue color. As the bird gets older the cere changes to the darker blue of the male or the reddish-brown of the female.

Budgies are very social creatures. In nature they congregate in flocks. A solitary bird kept in a cage therefore needs your attention and affection. This is also true of cockatiels and mynahs. While toys, swings, and bells in the cage help stave off boredom, these birds need company, too. They will repay your effort by being charming, affectionate companions.

A cage should be relatively uncluttered and large enough

This parakeet is making friends with an injured gray screech owl.

so your bird can exercise by flying from perch to perch. It is also a good idea to allow the budgies out of the cage for some part of each day. The exercise it gets by taking somewhat longer flights is beneficial.

Canaries seldom get tame enough to offer them the freedom of the house. These finches were first brought from the Canary Islands to Europe by the Spanish in the fifteenth century. Their joyful singing has made them popular all over the world.

Among the singing canaries there are two main types: choppers and rollers. The chopper has a loud and boisterous song, the roller a soft, melodic one. Male canaries are the singers, while females just chirp.

Although budgies usually live to be eight to ten years old, both canaries and budgies may live up to fifteen years in captivity. Perhaps we shouldn't call it captivity when we provide a protected home, freedom from predators, a balanced variety of foods, and affectionate care.

The general rules of housing, care, and feeding apply to all pet birds.

Taming and Training

A young budgie is easiest to tame and train, but with patience older birds can also become gentle pets. If you are shopping for a budgie, look for an individual that is bright, alert, sleek, and shiny. A young bird has dark eyes. The feathers on the forehead have dark stripes until the bird molts at ten to twelve weeks of age. By all means, if all things are equal, choose a young bird six to eight weeks of age. Start taming as soon as you bring your bird home. At that time it is unsure of itself and will readily accept your companionship and training.

One of the best ways to train your bird is by using food. Take the food out of the cage at night and then in the morning, when the young bird is hungry; offer a few seeds on the tip of your moistened finger through the side of the cage near the perch. If it won't accept them, put the food back in the cage and repeat the same thing the next morning.

When the budgie eats the first seed off your finger, you are on your way to winning. The next day do the same thing. The following day open the cage door and offer the seeds by placing your hand partially inside the cage. If it still eats from your finger, the next day place seeds in the palm of your hand and see if it will step on your hand to get the seeds. If the budgie does, it won't be long before it realizes you represent food, and it will look forward to seeing you at all times. While this could be called stomach training, a quicker, more direct training method is called finger training.

Finger training is especially effective if after three days the new budgie still refuses to accept food from your hand. For this, it is best to slow down your budgie by trimming its wings. This need not be a major trimming—just the painless removal of about three-quarters of an inch (2 cm) of the tips of the primary feathers of each wing.

You will need an assistant to hold the bird. Gently herd the budgie into one corner of the cage. Have your assistant grasp it as gently as possible around its body, confining both wings with the hand. Make sure the bird isn't squeezed, or it won't be able to breathe. A frightened bird usually tries to bite. If this worries the person holding the bird for you, have him or her wear light gloves. While your assistant holds the budgie, take hold of one wing and, with a sharp scissors, trim the tips of the long wing feathers off evenly. Repeat the procedure with the other wing. Place the bird on top of the cage and turn it loose.

Your budgie will still be able to fly, but not well. If it can fly well enough to make it difficult for you to catch it, trim another cm off the wings. It will require much more exertion for your budgie to fly short distances.

As soon as it lands, approach slowly, talking gently. As you move close, extend your hand and place one finger low against the bird's chest.

Budgie will either step on your finger or it will fly. If it flies, follow it and repeat the procedure. After two or three flights your budgie will be so tired it will not want to fly again and will step up onto your finger.

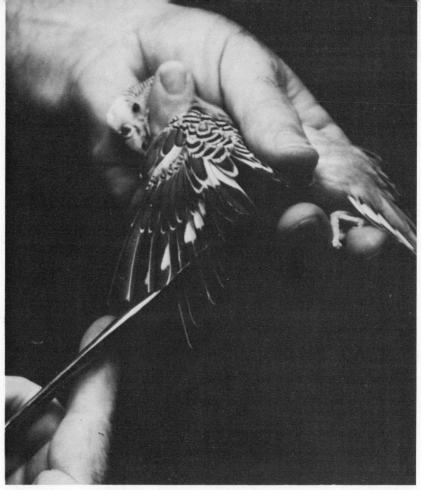

Wing feathers are trimmed to help finger train a bird.

Keep talking gently and reassuringly as you carry budgie back to its cage. Talk to it for a few minutes, then open the door and place your hand and the bird inside the cage. Your budgie will usually jump off your finger onto its favorite perch.

The following day open the cage door and let the budgie fly out of the cage. Pursue it slowly, talk to it gently, and persistently place your hand against its chest until it climbs on your finger. Carry it about on your finger for several minutes as you talk to it to reassure and calm it.

Raise your hand so the bird is level with your face. For some reason budgies like to watch your lips as you talk to them. They seem to grow calm watching and listening to you. After ten minutes of talking to your bird, put it back in the cage. Later in the day repeat the whole procedure two more times. Each time you convince the budgie to get on your finger makes the next time easier. Soon it looks forward to your coming; it enjoys being picked up and talked to. In just two or three days you can have your new bird finger-trained.

Occasionally, when you first start working with a frightened budgie, it may bite you. It can grasp a piece of skin in its small, strong beak, which can hurt. Try to ignore the pain. Once your bird learns that you aren't going to hurt it, it will stop trying to bite you.

If you slap at it or jerk your hand away when it bites, you will frighten the bird, and it will take that much longer to make it gentle. So if it bites you, grit your teeth, gently twist your finger to release it from the beak, and go right on with training. In a couple of days your budgie won't try to bite unless you try to restrain it by grabbing at its body.

Budgies, mynah birds, cockatiels, and parrots are about the only pets I know of that may answer back when you speak to them. For with a little patience on your part, they can be taught to mimic the human voice and many seem to give the proper response when you speak to them.

It is intriguing to listen to a talented talking bird, but it does require patience and perseverance to train a good talker. You must plan to devote at least twenty minutes twice a day to it.

Hold your finger-trained bird on your hand reasonably close to your face where it can watch you, and speak the phrase you wish it to learn. It should be a single word or a short phrase. It must be spoken clearly, concisely, and in the same tone of voice each time.

Repeat the phrase over and over and over for the entire period. Budgies find it easier to imitate a woman's or a young person's voice, rather than the deeper male voice.

If you are persistent, sooner or later the budgie will try to imitate you. It may take several days of training before it tries. When it does, repeat the word or phrase again, enunciating clearly to help the bird hear the little differences in the sounds of the words so it can imitate you.

When it learns one word or phrase and says it well, start on another. Start off each training session by going over the words and phrases the bird has already learned. When the review is completed to your satisfaction, introduce another word.

Soon you will hear budgie saying the words you have taught it as it plays or rests in its cage. Each time you hear it speak, reinforce the phrase by repeating it back to the bird.

Concentration and persistence are the factors that are required if your bird is to be a talented talker.

Housing

Most bird cages sold for budgies in pet shops are too small for your bird to get adequate exercise. Also, doors in the cage are too small to be able to withdraw your hand comfortably with a budgie on your finger. If, however, the cage is to be used only for eating and as a nighttime sleeping place, and the bird has the freedom of the house during the day, the average cage may be large enough.

In any event, it is easy to build a large cage that has all the room your bird needs. The two-foot cube (60 × 60 × 60 cm) cage shown in Chapter 13 works very well as a budgie cage. This cage would be large enough for a cockatiel or a mynah bird. A parrot would need a larger home.

Have the cage ready before you place your bird in it. Wire about three short branches in various parts of the cage for your bird to rest on and to fly to. Leave a clear space, so it has room to fly and exercise. Branches make good perches because they vary in diameter. This is better for your bird's feet than having all perches exactly the same size. You may also make a swing from a short branch and suspend it from the top of the cage.

Place newspaper in the bottom of the cage. Cut the papers to the size of the floor of the cage, and put a stack of them in the cage. Then each day the droppings and seed hulls can be removed by folding and lifting out the topmost paper.

Make a couple of simple wire brackets near one of the perches to hold seed and water dishes at the side of the cage. Place the dishes where it is convenient for you to reach through the cage to change them or to add food. Treat cups, which are small food dishes, a grit container, and a cuttle bone should be wired in place where the budgie can reach them.

Don't clutter the cage with toys, but do put several easily cleaned plastic toys where your bird can play with them. We have always given our budgies a mirror. A budgie spends a lot

A bell and mirror are a few of this parakeet's toys.

of time talking to that reflected image, but our birds always preferred to leave the cage and come to us when we opened the cage door.

Place the cage in a warm spot in the house where it won't be in a draft. The temperature of the average home is fine for most pet birds. While birds do need sunlight, don't place the cage where it receives direct sunlight over a period of several hours unless your bird has shade or can leave the cage. All birds enjoy sunbathing and basking in the sun, but when they get warm they need to get into the shade and cool down. Forcing it to stay in the sun can kill your bird.

You can tell if the temperature is right for your bird. If it is comfortable, the feathers of its body will be slicked down and the bird will have a sleek shape. If it is hot, the bird's wings droop and it pants by breathing with an open mouth. Move it to a cool spot at once.

If your bird is cool or chilled, it will sit with the feathers ruffled up. While a bird sleeps with its feathers ruffled up, that is not a normal condition when it is awake. If your bird is ruffled up, move the cage to a warmer spot in the house. Cover about half the cage with a cover to hold warmth in the cage area and supply extra heat.

You may place a heating pad under the cage, but we prefer to place a 40-watt light bulb outside the cage alongside the favorite perch. Your bird will move close to the bulb, absorbing the radiant warmth, just as you or I would in front of a fireplace. When it is warm enough it will move a comfortable distance away, but it will stay in the warmth. Leave the bulb burning night and day if your bird needs the extra warmth. Your budgie will sleep in spite of the light, and will be more comfortable in the warmth.

It is not necessary to cover your bird at night. We have never covered our budgies. A healthy bird adapts well to lower nighttime temperatures. The main thing is to be consistent. If you start covering your bird, do it every night; for a bird used to being covered may chill if exposed to a cooler temperature than it is accustomed to.

Feeding

The feeding of any pet bird is not difficult, and yet malnutrition is the single greatest disease problem we see in pet birds. As a general rule, your bird must have seeds, fresh green vegetables, additional minerals in a cuttle bone—obtainable at any pet supply store—or mineral block, supplemental treat food with added vitamins and trace elements, and fresh clean water. These general rules apply to all birds. The more detailed feeding of budgies follows.

The basic food of a budgie is its seeds. Basic "parakeet mix" consists of about 60 percent millet, 10 percent oats, and 30 percent canary seed. The millet seeds, round seeds, may be a mixture of red, white, and yellow. The canary seeds are oval in shape, while the hulled oats are longer, more cylindrical seeds. To be of maximum value as food, the seeds should be fresh and clean. When you open a box of seeds, smell them. They should smell similar to a loaf of bread, and not musty or moldy. All the seeds should look bright and shiny. If you have any doubt as to the freshness of the contents, run this test: Place a tablespoonful of seeds from the box on a damp paper towel on a regular dinner plate. Spread the seeds out evenly and cover them with another damp paper towel. Place the plate on the windowsill in the kitchen. Keep the paper towels damp. If you have good seed, practically all should show signs of sprouting in about three days.

Fresh parakeet mix must be placed in your bird's feed dish each day. The average budgie will eat about a teaspoonful of seeds daily. As a budgie eats, it hulls the seeds with its beak and tongue. Frequently the hulls fall back in the seed dish. What looks like a full dish may be primarily hulls, so inspect it closely, or else just routinely empty the dish and fill it each morning.

Since seeds and cereal grains are deficient in most minerals and low in vitamins A, B, C, and D, your budgie needs more than just seeds. It should be offered fresh fruit and a green leafy vegetable each day. A piece of lettuce, spinach, endive, carrot top, or even dandelion leaf is fine. Wash the greens before you place them in the cage to be sure any residual insecticides are removed. Budgies learn to enjoy oranges, bananas, grapes, apples, and just about any fruit you like.

Some people feel that adding greens to a bird's diet causes diarrhea. This is not true. If the bird hasn't been receiving greens regularly, it may overeat and this may cause a temporary diarrhea, but the condition will quickly correct itself. It is true that a bird eating greens daily has a more moist dropping than a bird not receiving greens. This is because the greens contain large amounts of water. This increased water intake will mean increased water excretion by the kidneys, so the droppings are more moist.

Fresh fruits not only provide a tasty variety to the diet, they add vitamins and minerals not found in the seeds. Offering a piece of fresh fruit each day will assure a variety of fruits over a week or a month's time. Each type of fruit provides its own unique combination of food elements, to ensure that your bird receives the nutrients it needs.

To be positive that no elements are overlooked, you can prepare a treat food for your pet bird that contains additional protein, vitamins, and other food elements. Grate a hard-boiled egg, crushing the egg shell as fine as possible. To the egg add a heaping teaspoonful of crushed dry Cat Chow or dry dog food and an equal amount of grated carrot. A teaspoonful of wheat germ and a teaspoonful of a good vitamin mineral powder for pets should also be added. Mix the ingredients well in a bowl by stirring with a fork. Place your treat mixture in a small jar with a top, and keep it in the refrigerator. Each day offer about a half teaspoonful of your treat mix in the treat cup.

A cuttle bone serves as an additional source of calcium. Chewing helps keep the beak worn down. While calcium is supplied in the egg shell and the vitamin mineral powder in your treat mix, it is a good idea to place a cuttlebone in the cage. You may tempt your bird to chew on the cuttlebone by making a couple of scratches on it with a sharp knife. Our birds never ate much of their cuttlebone. They apparently got all the calcium they needed from other items they ate.

Grit, which is small bits of crushed granite, should be placed in the cage, too. Grit functions as a grinding agent in the bird's gizzard, breaking down hard particles of food. Birds that hull their seeds seldom need grit, but budgies do eat it regularly. Choose mineralized grit. This is simply grit to which extra minerals are added. Don't put the grit on the bottom of the cage as many people do, for it becomes contaminated with fecal material. Rather, place it in a separate food dish near one of the perches.

If your mineralized grit does not contain iodine, this element should be given by adding a drop of iodine solution (Lugol's Solution) to the water dish twice weekly. The iodine solution may be obtained from a drugstore or from your veterinarian.

Additional vitamins should not be necessary if you are feeding the diet we have discussed here. If your bird is an older bird whose eating habits are well established and it refuses to change and eat the food it should, give extra vitamins. Be certain that soluble vitamins A and D_3 are included in the vitamin drops you select. In addition most liquid vitamins contain some of the B vitamins and trace minerals. It is easiest to give the vitamins by adding a drop to the bird's water each day. Place a drop on the seeds, also. As your bird picks up the seeds in its beak and rolls them around hulling them, some of the vitamins will come off in its mouth. But from all aspects the best source of vitamins is a balanced diet.

Many authorities recommend that you not allow your bird to eat any foods from your table. I disagree. Many of these foods are nutritious and add variety to your bird's diet. Naturally you must not allow your bird to forage around on your plate, but if it flies to the table in the morning, place a bit of buttered toast where your bird can eat it. Offer a bit of scrambled eggs whenever you have them. A green pea or a bit of squash is great at supper, and a tidbit of pound cake for dessert is easily digested and very nutritious for your pet.

Budgies have a high metabolic rate and require considerable food for their size. If a bird does not eat for a day, something is wrong. Some of them will die in forty-eight hours if they don't eat. If your bird is not eating, have it checked by your veterinarian as soon as possible.

Fortunately most budgies eat well and their natural curiosity will lead them to try any new foods you may offer. A bird that is an eager eater and that eats a variety of foods seldom has any dietary problems and is usually a healthy bird.

Canaries: These birds are fed a basic mixture of half canary seed and half rape seed. Check these seeds also for freshness and cleanliness. Offer your canary green vegetables, fruits, and the same homemade treat prepared for a budgie. In addition the canary must have grit.

Larger birds: Birds like cockatiels and mynahs should be offered a variety of foods, too. Along with its seeds, the *cockatiel* should have greens, fruit, peanut butter, bits of dry cat food, and other foods you find it likes. The *mynahs* should have the pelleted mynah food, treat food as prepared for budgies, grapes, bananas, apples, and other vegetables and fruits.

Parrots: These birds also require a variety of foods. Feed some of the larger seeds, such as pumpkin and sunflower, whole peanuts, sweet corn, apples, oranges, bananas, grapes, raisins, peas, carrots, lima beans, a piece of bread with peanut butter on it, and a couple of pieces of dry dog food. Peanut butter is an excellent food for most birds. It is tasty, rich in oils, high in calories, and is easily digested.

While parrots dearly love sunflower seeds, they have deficiency problems when they eat them to the exclusion of other foods. If you feed sunflower seeds, feed only a few each day as a treat and not as a basic diet.

All of the psittacine birds seem to enjoy chewing a fresh twig from a tree, such as maple, apple, or oak. It may be placed in the cage once or twice a week. Your bird will chew off bits of bark and leaves, and have a good time destroying the small branch.

All birds should have water available at all times. Budgies are desert birds and don't drink a lot. Usually a budgie will drink about a third of a teaspoonful (2 ml) a day. Since the average bird water dish holds over an ounce, the level will scarcely go down noticeably. Still, it is a good idea to remove the stale water every morning, rinse the waterer, and refill it with fresh clean water.

When your budgie is fed leafy green vegetables it may not drink much water. Because budgies drink so little water, it is not effective to add medication to water to treat them when they are sick.

It is, however, an effective way to give vitamins and the iodine because only tiny amounts are required by your bird. In fact all pet birds should receive iodine in their water twice weekly. Just add two drops of the iodine solution (p. 191) to the water when you change it.

Water may be provided for bathing, too. Many of the budgies, and other birds, enjoy a bath several times a week. Place a saucer of water over a couple of absorbent paper towels on the floor of the cage.

When your budgie discovers it, it will fly down to investigate. Most will stand on the edge of the saucer and timidly place their beak in the water and flick a few drops about. As their enthusiasm grows, they begin wading in the water, fluffing their feathers up, working droplets of water among the feathers, and shaking water everywhere.

It is enjoyable to watch the fun these little birds get from the simple pleasure of a bath. Some birds never learn to bathe, but the majority will enjoy it.

Breeding

Perhaps someday you will desire to breed and raise budgies or other pet birds. The cage described in Chapter 13 will be fine as a breeding cage.

Prepare the cage as described in the section on housing, except add a nest box. This should be made of wood, and—for a budgie—have inside base dimensions six by six inches (15 × 15 cm) and be eight inches (20 cm) tall. The bottom board should be fashioned with a saucerlike depression in the center so the eggs will not roll about. A two-inch (5 cm) hole is drilled about two-thirds of the way up one of the side walls. This is the entrance for the birds.

A male (blue cere) and female (reddish-brown cere) are placed in the cage. If you have more than one pair of birds, each pair should have its own cage. Budgies are mature enough to breed at ten months of age. Most breeding and egg laying will take place in the spring and early summer.

A hen will lay four to six eggs in the nest box. She lays one egg every other day. The hen will do all the incubating of the eggs during the eighteen days until they hatch. The male will frequently feed her as she sits on the eggs.

When the eggs hatch, the naked, blind, helpless babies are fed by both the parents. The babies quickly learn to take re-gurgitated, partially digested food, along with digestive tract secretions, from a parent's mouth.

At ten days the fast-growing babies can see and are starting to have feathers. By four or five weeks of age they are fully feathered. At six weeks they can be taken from the parents, for they are eating well and capable of looking after themselves.

There can be some problems associated with breeding budgies. Sometimes a pair will live together happily but will not breed. You may have to get another pair of birds. While a solitary pair may not breed, two or more pairs in sight of each other usually breed readily.

Occasionally a female breeds, but cannot pass the egg. This is called egg-bound and is a serious situation. The problem is discussed under diseases, since it is also a problem in nonbreeding females.

It is very unlikely that both parents would die and leave you faced with raising orphan budgies. However, if it were to happen, the babies would have to be taken from the nest box and reared in an open nest where you could care for them.

They would need extra warmth, which is most easily provided by hanging a 40-watt bulb close to the nest. Check the temperature in the nest. It should be 95°F (35°C) for very young birds. Each week, as the babies grow feathers and are able to provide their own warmth, you can lower the nest temperature five F degrees (three C degrees).

To feed young orphans, use a mixture of a tablespoonful (15 cc) of high protein baby cereal, one third of a hard-boiled egg yolk, a quarter teaspoonful (1 cc) of a vitamin mineral powder, and enough water to make a thick liquid mixture.

Use a medicine dropper to place bite-sized portions in the babies' beaks. When they find out it is food and make the effort to reach and take it from you, start offering it in a teaspoon. Bend the sides of the spoon upward to make a deeper trough. This makes it easier for the babies to eat.

As the babies grow older, place bits of grit and crushed seeds in the mixture. When they are ten days old place a dish of the homemade treat mixture so that it is available to the babies at all times. Gradually, as the young budgies become better able to fend for themselves, offer seeds and other foods.

The care of other psittacine orphans would be very similar to that of budgies, and equally as unlikely to be necessary. For even if one parent bird died, the remaining parent would feed and care for the babies and do all the work for you.

Raising baby birds can be fun, if you have made some arrangements to sell them. With many birds to care for, they will no longer be pets, but work. You will lose the fun of knowing your individual birds well, and they are deprived of your companionship.

Diseases

How do you know when your bird is sick? What do you look for to decide if you need to consult a veterinarian?

Generally a sick bird talks or sings less than normal. It is droopy, listless, and sleeps a good deal of the time. It eats less and drinks less.

The droppings of a healthy bird are a circle of dark gray-black pasty material with a central white spot of kidney secretion. A normal bird will eliminate thirty to forty times daily.

Fewer droppings are not a direct sign of disease, but they do indicate a lower, or decreased, food intake. Any bird which has less than twenty droppings a day is a sick bird.

Seeds in the droppings indicate digestion is not taking place properly. Greenish droppings indicate an intestinal upset or infection. Whenever there is a marked change in consistency or number of droppings, a veterinarian should be consulted.

If your bird sits on the perch with its feathers ruffled, it is chilled. This frequently is associated with a fever. Wheezing, clicking noises or whistles when your bird breathes, nasal discharges, bubbles from the nostrils in the cere, flying or walking abnormally, and not eating are all serious symptoms. Your bird needs veterinary help.

Until you can take your bird in to the veterinary hospital for examination, there are several things you should do. Place a thermometer in the cage. Cover three sides of the cage with clear plastic wrap. This will stop drafts and hold in the warmth. The clear plastic allows you to watch your bird and, with one side open, to change food dishes without uncovering your bird. Place a heating pad under the cage or a light bulb outside the cage close to a favorite perch. The bulb should be on the side not covered by the clear plastic wrap. Your bird will snuggle up to the light, soaking up the radiant warmth. Keep the bulb or heating pad on at all times, and be certain you keep the temperature inside the cage at 85°F to 90°F (29°–32°C).

Allow your bird to rest, but tempt it to eat by placing fresh food in the cage. Offer its favorite foods placed close by the perch. Keep fresh water available at all times.

If possible, a sick bird should be transported to the veterinary hospital in its regular cage. The cage should not be cleaned, so your veterinarian can examine the number and characteristics of the droppings. Cover the cage or leave the plastic wrap around it, but empty the water dish so it doesn't spill. Bring any medication or vitamins you are giving along with you.

Diarrhea or Bloody Droppings: Loose bowel movements that occur without any changes in the diet are usually due to infection. While blood in the bowel movement can indicate other problems, it usually indicates a severe and serious infection. Your veterinarian should examine your bird.

Provide extra warmth as soon as you notice the diarrhea.

Do not remove the green vegetables from the diet. Do offer soft easily digested foods, such as mashed hard-boiled egg yolk, high-protein baby cereal, or even pound cake. In addition, offer the usual variety of foods.

Give a kaolin-pectin or bismuth suspension, both of which can be obtained at the drugstore. Give two or three drops twice daily with a medicine dropper.

To give the medication hold the bird gently in one hand in an upright position. Using a medicine dropper, place a drop on the bird's tongue.

If the diarrhea is caused by an infection, your veterinarian will probably give your bird an injection of antibiotics. In addition he may prescribe additional medication for you to give.

The Hartz Mountain Corporation has a product for budgies called Keet Life. It is a mixture of seeds that have been impregnated with the antibiotic Chlortetracycline. This product is effective and may be used if your bird is still eating. No other food should be offered except the Keet Life seed mixture during the ten to fourteen day treatment period.

If your bird is not eating well, the antibiotics must be given by injection or by stomach tube. If the medication is to be given by stomach tube, your veterinarian will show you how to do it.

Adding antibiotics to the drinking water is not a reliable way to treat a budgie. They drink so little water you can never be sure they are receiving an adequate amount of the medication. Other birds drink more water and may be treated by adding antibiotics to the drinking water.

Since most budgies spit out a portion of any medication you give with a dropper, it is difficult to know when enough has been given.

Sinusitis and Upper Respiratory Infection: With this infection your bird will sneeze and have a mucous discharge from the nostril openings in the cere. It will be depressed and sit with its feathers ruffled. Because this is a bacterial infection, these birds should be treated by providing extra warmth and antibiotics for ten to fourteen days. If your bird is eating, the Keet Life (Hartz) may be used. If it is not eating well, consult your veterinarian.

Psittacosis (Parrot Fever): This is a contagious disease of psittacine birds that can infect people. Most imported birds are treated to eliminate this disease when they enter this country. While there has been a steady decline in the number of human cases in the last twenty years, there are still a number of cases diagnosed every year in birds.

In man the disease is an influenzalike disease with fever, chills, headache, cough, and vomiting. In birds the symptoms are not specific either. In the budgie, it generally appears as an upper respiratory disease with sneezing, nasal discharge, raspy breathing, diarrhea, poor appetite, and frequently, sudden death.

Psittacosis cannot be positively diagnosed either by examination, clinical symptoms, or by an autopsy examination. If the symptoms and autopsy findings suggest psittacosis, your veterinarian will send blood and tissue specimens to a laboratory for further examination.

Over 70 percent of the birds sold through retail sales are given some preventative treatments before they are offered for sale. If you are unable to find out where your bird came from, or whether it has had this preventative treatment, I would suggest you give it yourself.

Chlortetracycline is the antibiotic used to eliminate this disease. For budgies, give the Keet Life (Hartz) seeds, which contain chlortetracycline, as the only food for forty-five days. For larger psittacine birds and parrots, add 500 mg chlortetracycline to a pint (480 ml) of water and give this solution as the drinking water for a month. Make up a new stock solution as needed, and keep it in the refrigerator. Each day discard the drinking water in the cage, rinse the water dish, and refill the water dish with the stock solution. (This antibiotic solution may be used to treat other bacterial infections in these birds, also.)

Since psittacosis has declined in people to less than fifty cases a year, it is not a widespread disease. Budgies were involved in very few of these cases. And yet we should do our part to reduce the number of cases.

Give your bird the preventative treatment if you are not sure where it was bred or where it came from. Consult your veterinarian if your bird shows any of the symptoms listed, and request an autopsy if it dies suddenly.

Molting Problems: Budgies normally molt for the first time when they are ten to twelve weeks old. You will notice feathers strewn about on the floor of the cage. The spikes of the solid colored new feathers are most noticeable on the forehead of your bird. This loss of feathers is normal, and you may expect your bird to repeat this molting once or twice each year for the rest of its life.

Canaries usually molt in spring and fall, while the budgies are more irregular, but usually get new feathers once a year. Some birds molt a little bit all year long.

Some budgies don't molt. Due to poor nutrition and a hormone imbalance, they don't shed the worn feathers as they should. The feather colors get dull, the tips become frayed, and the bird looks shabby.

If your bird doesn't molt, or doesn't complete the molting process in thirty to forty days, you probably have a nutritional problem as well as a hormone imbalance. Correct the diet by offering the foods, treat, and other items listed under feeding. If there is no improvement in thirty days, contact your veterinarian.

Most frequently the hormone testosterone is needed. We usually prepare a solution with 100 mg of the testosterone in an ounce (30 ml) of water. Two drops of this solution are placed in the drinking water each day. When male canaries won't sing after they finish molting, the same hormone is dispensed to them the same way.

Molting is always a time of stress for your bird, but it is a normal situation that is triggered by the length of the day and environmental temperatures. At no time during molting is your bird unable to fly.

There is a specific disease of young budgies called French molt. When the young bird molts, the primary wing feathers and the tail feathers don't come back in. While these birds flutter about, they can't fly. This disease is believed to be a combination of an inherited disease and a nutritional situation. There is no treatment except to feed the best diet you can, and hope.

Broken Feathers: A broken feather will continue to bleed until it is removed, then the hemorrhage stops. A new feather will not grow in until the damaged feather has been removed. The feather should be pulled in the direction it is growing. Do not pull more than one feather at a time, or you may exert enough force to tear the skin.

Flight feathers and tail feathers may be difficult to pull out. It may require the use of a forceps, and sometimes an anesthetic is required. If you can't remove the feather with your fingers, ask your veterinarian to help.

Feather Picking: Sometimes a bored budgie will start picking at its feathers and pulling them out. While preening and grooming are normal, a bird usually does not remove feathers in patches.

Provide more freedom and exercise. Place a few new toys in the cage and make certain you are feeding a variety of foods. Most feather picking in mynah birds appears to be due to malnutrition rather than boredom as it is in budgies.

Goiter-Iodine Deficiency: Iodine deficiency is seen regularly in budgies and parrots. The deficiency causes an enlargement of the thyroid glands, which are found on either side of the neck. This swelling interferes with swallowing and causes a squeak with each respiration.

Prevention is the same as treatment. You may obtain two ounces (60 ml) of Lugol's Solution, which is 10 percent iodine, from the drugstore. Take 2 ml of this solution and add it to one ounce (30 ml) of water in a dropper bottle. Each day place a drop or two in the water in your budgie's water dish. For a larger bird measure how much water the water dish holds. Give two drops of the mixture for each ounce of water in the dish.

Calcium Deficiency: Birds fed primarily just seeds suffer some calcium deficiency. Parrots fed on a diet of sunflower seeds and/or peanuts will show severe deficiency signs. The birds have soft, rubbery bones that fracture easily. They don't fly well and are weak. As the disease progresses, you may see them have seizures or convulsions, or you may just find your bird dead.

It is imperative that the birds be fed a balanced diet. Calcium gluconate tablets or dicalcium phosphate capsules can be dissolved in water and given as the drinking water. Soluble vitamin preparations containing vitamin D_3 should be added to the water also.

While it may take some time, offer other foods and restrict sunflower seeds until one day you offer just a couple now and then as a treat.

Scaly Face and Leg Mites: The tiny mites causing this condition live in the tissue at the base of the beak and under the scales on the legs. They cause an irritation that makes the beak look porous and distorted, and makes it grow crooked. As the disease progresses scaly material forms about the side of the face and the cere. The legs also look rough and scaly.

The treatment must kill the mites, but not the bird. A salve that is safe to use may be obtained from your veterinarian. He will show you how to apply it to the scaly spots with your fingertips. It must be rubbed into the spots twice weekly for a month.

Feather Mites, Lice, Ticks: You may see lice on your bird, or tiny red mites crawling on the perches at night, or tiny black mites moving on the ends of a perch during the day, but all of these are relatively uncommon. If your bird scratches often and you suspect parasites of this type, hang a Shell pest strip close to the cage for eight hours each day at a time when your bird is in the cage. Do this twice weekly for three weeks. This will kill any mites, lice, or ticks in the cage or on the bird.

Gout: This is a fairly common problem in budgies. Gout is the deposit of uric acid crystals in a joint. The cause of this condition is unknown. The primary symptom is pain. The budgie will move from foot to foot restlessly, and may even lie in the bottom of the cage.

If the joints in the leg are examined closely, the small yellow-white nodules of uric acid can be seen under the skin.

Treatment is not very effective. Your veterinarian can remove the nodules surgically, but they usually return. You may put a regular five grain aspirin tablet in eight ounces (240 ml) of water to use as the drinking water to help control the pain. If the budgie is in pain most of the time, euthanasia is probably the most humane course to follow.

Tumors: Tumors are common in older budgies. Some can be removed surgically if they are discovered before they become too large. Any unusual lumps you notice on your bird should be examined by your veterinarian.

Vomiting: In budgies this is not usually a sign of disease. In courtship the budgie offers food to its mate in this way. It will also offer it to its reflected image in the mirror. If it persists, remove the mirror from the cage. If it still persists, have your bird examined.

Fractures, Bruises, and Concussions: Leg fractures should be placed in a Scotch tape splint, while wing fractures are usually treated by taping the wing in a normal position, using the feathers as splints. If you are not sure of what you are doing, let your veterinarian help you.

Budgies sometimes fly into a window or mirror, causing a head injury and concussion. It may be unconscious or partially paralyzed. It is best to keep the budgie quiet and warm. Place it in the bottom of the cage, place the cage on a heating pad, and cover it. Place a thermometer near your bird, and be sure the temperature does not go above 95°F (35°C). If it isn't greatly improved in several hours, have it examined.

Long Beaks or Nails: Both upper and lower beaks grow continuously. Normally the wear of chewing keeps them at the proper length. If the beak does seem to be growing too long, have your veterinarian show you how to trim it.

Toenails, too, sometimes need trimming. You can see the pink of the blood vessels through the transparent nails. Don't cut into this pink area, for the nail will bleed.

If you make a mistake and cut the nail too short, it will seldom bleed for long. If several drops of blood are lost, hold the bird in one hand and place a fingertip against the end of the bleeding nail for four or five minutes to stop further blood loss and to allow a firm clot to form.

Ask your veterinarian to show you how to trim the nails.

Egg-Bound: Females will sometimes lay eggs even if a male is not present. Sometimes the egg will not pass, because it is too large or the female is too small. The female will stand upright like a penguin, and you can see and feel the egg in the abdomen.

If the egg doesn't pass out in an hour, the bird needs help. Several drops of mineral oil should be released from a medicine dropper into the vent. Place the bird in a warm cage. Frequently with this lubrication the egg will be eliminated. If it hasn't passed in an hour repeat the instillation of the mineral oil and, with gentle pressure, use your fingertips to move the egg toward the vent. If this doesn't work, the egg probably will have to be surgically removed. Don't wait. Consult your veterinarian, for an egg-bound hen will die in a few hours.

With all these diseases and problems listed, it would appear that budgies are in trouble or sick most of the time. This is not true. Most budgies are remarkably healthy.

Since nutritional deficiencies are a contributing cause in many of these problems, prevention is more important than treatment. A healthy bird is one that is fed a good diet with a variety of foods offered, including fresh fruits and vegetables. If your budgie is provided a good home in a draft-free area of the house, given the chance to exercise, and provided with the companionship of you as a friend, I am sure your bird will be healthy.

References and Suggested Reading

Bates, Henry J., and Robert Brusenback. *Parrots and Related Birds.* Jersey City: T. F. H. Publications, Inc., 1967.

Brownell, J. R. *Diagnosis and Treatment of Caged Bird Diseases in the Veterinary Practice.* Ames: Iowa State University Press, 1968.

Dolensek, E. P., and Barbara Burn. *A Practical Guide to Impractical Pets.* New York: Viking Press, 1976.

Dolphin, R. E. "Hospital Care for Birds," in *Veterinary Medicine/Small Animal Clinician,* April 1977, pp. 641–642.

Dolphin, R. E., and D. E. Olsen. "Psittacosis and Resistant Infections in Companion Birds," *Veterinary Medicine/Small Animal Clinician,* January 1977, pp. 70–74.

Lafeber, T. J. "Examination, Medication Techniques and Hospitalization for Parakeet and Canary," *Current Veterinary Therapy,* vol. V. Philadelphia: W. B. Saunders, 1974.

Lafeber, T. J. "Feather Disorders of Common Caged Birds," in *Current Veterinary Therapy,* vol. V. Philadelphia: W. B. Saunders, 1974.

Martin, Sharon L. *Notes on Caged Birds.* Columbus: Ohio State University, College of Veterinary Medicine, 1977.

Wallach, J. D., and A. A. Flieg. "Nutritional Hyperparathy-
roidism in Captive Psittacine Birds," *Journal of the American Veterinary Medical Association*, vol. 151, no. 7,
October 1, 1967.

The Final Goal

"O, yet we trust that somehow good
Will be the final goal of ill,
To pangs of nature, sins of will,
Defects of doubt and taints of blood;

That nothing walks with aimless feet;
That not one life shall be destroyed,
Or cast as rubbish to the void,
When God hath made the pile complete;

That not a worm is cloven in vain,
That not a moth with vain desire
Is shrivelled in a fruitless fire,
Or but subserves another's gain."

Tennyson. *In Memoriam*, I, iii.

13 / How to Build a Cage

A. *List of Materials*
1. ⅜″ or ½″ thick exterior plywood sheeting, 2′ × 4′
2. Hardware cloth ½″ mesh, 24″ wide, 10′ long
3. Fine wire 22 gauge, 20′ long
4. 1″ × 2″ boards, 14′ long
5. Small pair of hinges
6. 1 dozen 1¼″ screws
7. Hook-and-eye latch
8. Assorted nails
9. Woodworking glue
10. Spray paint

B. *Tools Required*
1. Hammer
2. Saw
3. Square—or ruler and straightedge

4. Tin snips (to cut hardware-cloth)
5. Screwdriver
6. Drill for screw holes (not required but does help)
7. Pliers

C. *Directions for Construction*

Divide 24″ × 48″ plywood in half. One half will be the base or floor. Divide the other half into four pieces 6″ wide. Leave two 24″ long. Cut the other two down to 23½″. The four pieces will be attached to the base and will make up part of the sides.

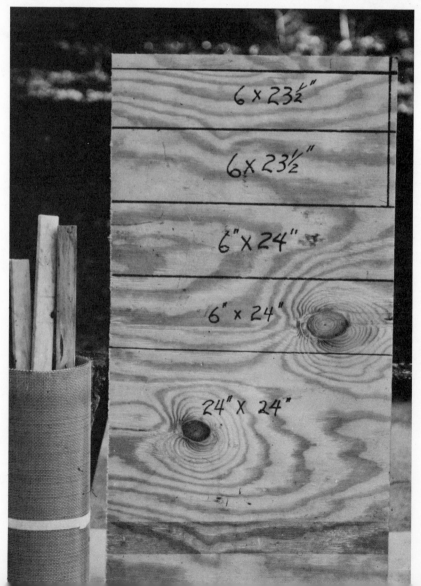

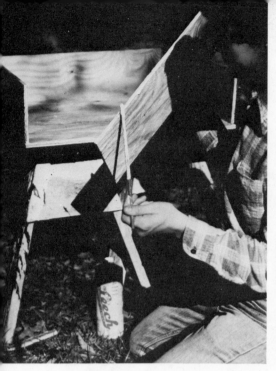

Take the four pieces and glue them to the base by spreading glue on the edges of the sides where they contact the base and each other.

Nail the sides to the base and to each other with 6 penny box nails. (Any nail about 2″ long will work.)

Seal all joints and cracks with glue.

To measure hardware-cloth, hold it up to base and make the first fold equal to the inside length of the wooden side. Bend all four sides to fit the base, allowing two-inch overlap at the starting corner. Cut off and save the excess material. It will be used to make the top.

Insert wire into base to be certain it fits properly.

Lace up the open corner with fine wire, beginning at the bottom edge. Cut a hole with your tin snips in one side for a door. Save the hardware-cloth for your door. (We usually make our door about 12″ square.)

Make an inner and outer frame on both sides of the wire from 1″ × 2″ wide lumber. Alternate your boards, so that the joints of both frames are in different spots. This will make the frame firm and rigid.

See that the hardware-cloth lies snugly between both frames, and screw outer frame to inner frame.

The door is made of the same material as the frame. Measure the height and width, so your door fits within the frame. We use long screws in the corners of the door to make it more rigid. (It helps to drill a hole slightly smaller than the screw you use, as you assemble the door. This helps keep the wood from splitting.)

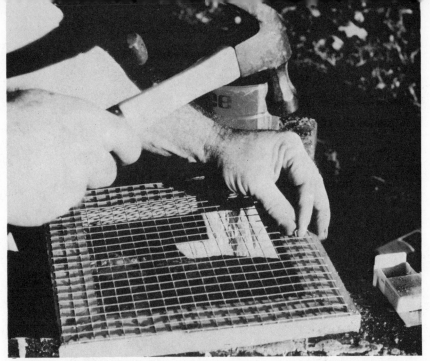

Tack the small piece of hardware-cloth to the inside of the door.

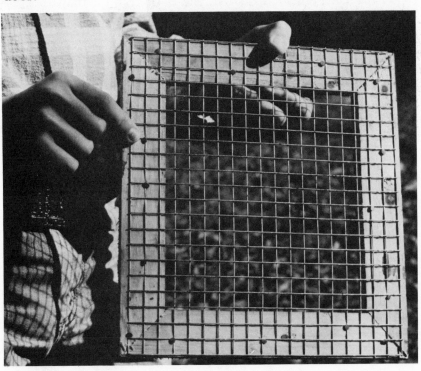

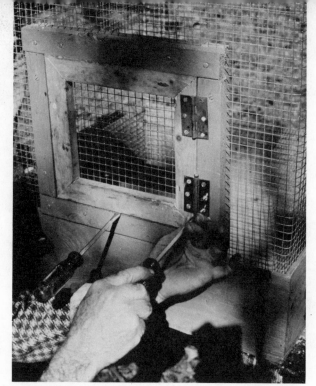

Fasten the finished door to the door frame with two small hinges.

The remaining hardware-cloth for the top is bent to give an overlap wherever possible where it meets the sides. This makes the whole cage more rigid.

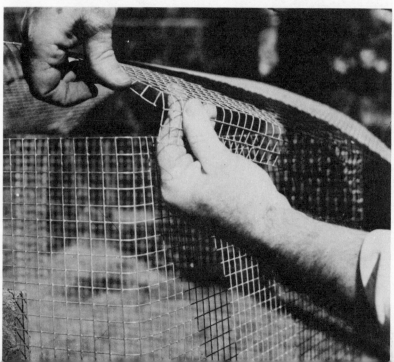

Lace the top to the sides with fine wire.

A hook on the door and a touch of spray paint complete the cage.

Total working time is two to four hours, depending on your skill. Total cost is under twenty dollars, depending on where you live.

Definitions

Cesarean section: The surgical removal of the unborn young from the mother's uterus.

Carnivorous: Those organisms that feed on animal tissue.

Coprophagy: The eating of fecal material. This is a method of recycling to obtain additional nutrients practiced normally by some rodents.

Euthanasia: Causing death painlessly to prevent suffering.

Gestation period: The interval from the time of fertilization to birth or hatching.

Habitat: The place where an organism normally lives.

Herbivorous: Those organisms that feed primarily on plant material.

Metamorphosis: A major change in form during the development from egg through intermediate stages to adult.

Omnivorous: Those organisms that eat both plant and animal material.

Ovulation: The release of eggs from the ovaries.

Prescription Drugs: Drugs, that because of their potential to do harm if misused, are controlled and dispensed only on prescription by a veterinarian, physician or dentist.

Prolific: Capable of producing large numbers of young.

Psittacine birds: Members of the Parrot family. A group of birds found in many areas of the world. They are characterized by strong hooked beaks, malletlike tongues, and strong legs for climbing. The group includes parrots, lories, lorikeets, cockatoos, cockatiels, macaws, and more than twenty types of parakeets, of which the budgerigar is one.

Index

About the Author

William J. Weber, DVM, is a veterinarian with over thirty years of experience in private practice in Leesburg, Florida. The Weber family home is in the midst of a lakeshore wildlife sanctuary.

Dr. Weber's writing and photographs appear regularly in wildlife and nature magazines. He is the author of *Wild Orphan Babies, Wild Orphan Friends,* and *Attracting Birds and Other Wildlife to Your Yard.*